ALL OUT FOR ONE

Cricket has been a lifelong fascination for author, commentator and after-dinner speaker Ken Piesse, born the year the MCG wicket was illegally watered in 1955.

He stayed home from school to compile his first book of cricket statistics, did dawn paper-rounds to finance book purchases and, when he wasn't playing or practising, would be found at the MCG, watching.

Ken has edited cricket magazines since 1978, commentated on the game on radio since 1980, and written over 40 books – including *Cricket's Colosseum: 125 Years of Test Cricket at the MCG*, the famous club's first official Test history. His Cameron White interview, for Fox Sports' *Inside Cricket*, won a major award from Cricket Victoria in 2001–02. Previously, he won the Victorian Cricket Association's overall media award for a two-part feature on Shane Warne. He is a member of the Melbourne Cricket Club's Media Hall of Fame.

Ken is married and has five children, two dogs and two cats. He and wife, Susan, hosted a supporters' tour to England in 2005.

email: kenpiesse@ozemail.com.au
web site: www.cricketbooks.com.au

Cricket books by Ken Piesse

Great Triumphs in Test Cricket (1978)
Prahran Cricket Club Centenary History (1978)
Cricket Digest Annual (ed.) (1980)
Cricket Year Annual (ed.) (1980–83)
Calypso Summers (with Jim Main) (1981)
The Great Australian Book of Cricket Stories (1982)
The Golden Age of Australian Cricket (ed.) (1982)
Duel for Glory: England Tours of Australia 1861–1982
(with Jim Main) (1982)
Donald Bradman (Famous Australians series) (1983)
Cartoonists at the Cricket (ed.) (1983)
The A to Z of Cricket (1983)
Bradman and the Bush (with Ian Ferguson) (1986)
Hooked on Cricket (with Max Walker) (1988)
Match Drawn (ed.) (1988)
Simply the Best: The Allan Border Story (1993)
Warne: Sultan of Spin (1995)
Cricket Skill and Secrets (1995–99)
One-Day Magic (1996)
The Big Australian Cricket Book (1996)
Wildmen of Cricket Vol. 1 (with Brian Hansen) (1998)
T.J. Over the Top (with Terry Jenner) (1999)
The Taylor Years (1999)
Steve and Mark Waugh (2000)
Cricket's Greatest Scandals (2000)
The Complete Shane Warne (2000)
The Waugh Zone (2001)
Retired Hurt (with Roshan Mahanama) (2001)
Bradmans of the Bush (with Alf Wilson) (2002)
Glenn McGrath and Adam Gilchrist (2003)
Cricket's Colosseum: 125 Years of Test Cricket
at the MCG (2003)
Down at the Junction: St Kilda's First 150 Years (2005)

ALL OUT FOR ONE

and Other Cricket Anecdotes

KEN PIESSE

Foreword by Darren Lehmann

VIKING
an imprint of
PENGUIN BOOKS

Every effort has been made to locate the copyright holders of printed and photographic material in this book, and the publisher welcomes hearing from anyone in this regard.

VIKING

Published by the Penguin Group
Penguin Group (Australia)
250 Camberwell Road, Camberwell, Victoria 3124, Australia
(a division of Pearson Australia Group Pty Ltd)
Penguin Group (USA) Inc.
375 Hudson Street, New York, New York 10014, USA
Penguin Group (Canada)
10 Alcorn Avenue, Toronto, Ontario, Canada M4V 3B2 (a division of Pearson Penguin Canada Inc.)
Penguin Books Ltd
80 Strand, London WC2R 0RL, England
Penguin Ireland
25 St Stephen's Green, Dublin 2, Ireland (a division of Penguin Books Ltd)
Penguin Books India Pvt Ltd
11 Community Centre, Panchsheel Park, New Delhi – 110 017, India
Penguin Group (NZ)
Cnr Airborne and Rosedale Roads, Albany, Auckland, New Zealand
(a division of Pearson New Zealand Ltd)
Penguin Books (South Africa) (Pty) Ltd
24 Sturdee Avenue, Rosebank, Johannesburg 2196, South Africa

Penguin Books Ltd, Registered Offices: 80 Strand, London, WC2R 0RL, England

First published by Penguin Group (Australia), a division of Pearson Australia Group Pty Ltd, 2005

10 9 8 7 6 5 4 3 2 1

Design by George Dale © Penguin Group (Australia)
Colour reproduction by Splitting Image Colour Studio Pty Ltd, Clayton, Victoria
Typeset in Sabon 12/14 pt by Midland Typesetters, Maryborough, Victoria
Printed and bound in Australia by McPherson's Printing Group, Maryborough, Victoria

National Library of Australia
Cataloguing-in-Publication data:

Piesse, Ken.
All out for one and other cricket anecdotes.
Bibliography.
Includes index.
ISBN 0 670 04275 7.
1. Cricket – Australia – Anecdotes. 2. Cricket – Humor. I.
Title.
796.3580994

www.penguin.com.au

foreword

IIIIIIIIIII

All Out for One . . . It's an appealing title for cricketers of all denominations, and triggers a multitude of memories for me – good and bad. Thankfully, even in the juniors at Whyalla South, we were never dismissed for less than double figures. But in a club match in Melbourne, years ago, we were all out for 36 and, like most of Carlton's first XI that day, I made a duck. Then there was the time Joe Scuderi took six for 6 to help us dismiss the Wackers for 41 in a Shield game in Adelaide. It was a performance that all but got him a tour of England.

Amazing feats and tall tales are part and parcel of cricket. You never forget the big moments, like Punter's huge sixes in the World Cup final at Jo'burg, or Hookesy hitting five fours in a row off Tony Greig in the Centenary Test. Talk about inspired! I was only seven at the time but I marched out into the backyard, swinging like nobody's business. It's amazing that the windows survived, let alone Mum's prized Cecil Brunners. In those days, every kid I knew played cricket in summer and footy in winter. It was sport 24/7. But cricket was king. We'd watch the Tests on TV with the sound off, so the ads didn't interrupt too much. On weekends and in the holidays, we'd play street games until the sun went down.

My 12-year-old son, Jake, made his first century the other day. He had a smile as wide as the Adelaide Oval, especially when I told him my first ton didn't come until I was 13. One thing he didn't do was get down on his hands and knees and kiss the old malthoid wicket, like I did at Gawler South. Not until that day had it dawned on me that perhaps I could make something of myself in the game.

Twenty years or so later, I'm just as passionate about it, even if the reflexes have dimmed a little and I've long stopped worrying about my body shape. At 35, you no longer have anything to prove. There's no pressure. The team is like an extended family. Everyone is thick and we like to keep it that way – even if the oldies like Warnie and I have no idea about the musical tastes of Watto and the Pup. (It must be said, however, that the music has improved since Steve Waugh retired. And Brett Lee insists he's going to move on from Ronan Keating ballads next time he jumps up on a bar after a win.)

My favourite memories? Well, Jason Gillespie had been promising something special if he ever got a Test 50. To see him finally celebrate the event, in late 2004, by riding his bat down the centre of the 'Gabba like Adam Sandler in *Happy Gilmore* was certainly worth the wait. And I could tell stories about Brad Hogg and Andrew Symonds until the cows come home. Passing Royal Randwick on our way into town from Sydney Airport one day, Hoggy asked, 'Is that where they hold the Melbourne Cup?' Simmo even topped that one, though, when he bought a raffle ticket at a function one evening. On being told the raffle would be drawn on the 31st, he responded, 'Well then . . . I'll expect a call on the 32nd!'

The fact that cricket is now a multimillion-dollar business doesn't mean that you're not allowed to laugh any more. It annoys me that, as international cricketers, we're often typecast and not allowed to be ourselves. I'd rather see people enjoying themselves. It's one of the reasons that I believe Twenty20 cricket has a place. It's three hours of fun – you just go out there and have a real lash. As long as we treat it as fun, it'll continue to prosper;

if we take it too seriously, it might flounder. The fans want to see sixes – the bigger the better. When I dobbed a couple over the Victor Richardson Gates, I immediately thought I was Hookesy. But not once, as Greg Blewett loves to remind me, have I been able to clear the straight-hit fence at either end in Adelaide. Despite his pencil-thin build, he has – and he hasn't shut up since!

I've always considered myself lucky to call Adelaide home and the Adelaide Oval my backyard. I have so many fond memories there. Sometimes I'll sit down on the Hill after training and listen to the midday church bells. When the sun is shining and you're taking in the smell of the just-cut outfield, there's nothing better. It's one of the reasons why old cricketers want to keep going, and put off a cricketing afterlife for as long as possible.

Before finishing, may I congratulate the author, who has been writing longer than I've been playing. Ken tells me this is his forty-first book. He showed me the player-by-player stats he keeps each summer, and has done for nigh on forty years. It shows a great passion for the game. Few match his knowledge or have his rapport with the players. It's been a privilege to contribute these few words. I trust that this latest book is also a raging success.

Keep Smiling :)

DARREN LEHMANN
Adelaide, June 2005

preface

IIIIIIIIIIII

It was my first Test at the Sydney Cricket Ground and my first time in the old press box, perched high up at the back of the M. A. Noble Stand. Keen to be in the front row and up close and personal with the scorers, I was an hour early and still taking in the ambience and atmosphere when in walked the tall, silver-headed, unmistakeable figure of Bill 'Tiger' O'Reilly.

Eyeing me in his favourite seat, he boomed, 'I've only been sitting in this same seat now for 37 years. And buggered if I'm going to be moving . . . Where are you from, son? . . . Ahh, Melbourne – it figures.'

The scorer, Ernie Cosgrove, smiled as my complexion slowly returned from a beetroot red and I recomposed myself, having shifted a few seats over.

'I-I-I'm Ken Piesse,' I said.

'Yes, Ken. Bill O'Reilly,' he said, offering his hand and regaling me with the first of what turned out to be dozens of striking anecdotes – from meeting Henry Lawson as a kid to how sectarianism permeated cricket, and what he *really* thought about the Don. Afterwards, I calculated I'd learnt more in eight hours than in my entire six years at Beaumaris High. I couldn't tell you who batted first that day – but I *had* met the Tiger!

A platoon of journalists followed the Test matches around then (the early eighties). Every paper in every capital city had its own match reporter, and the majors also had their side-bar or 'colour' man like Tiger, who'd been writing for the *Sydney Morning Herald* since the late forties. He'd write his stories in a VANA exercise book shortly before teatime, dictate them to a copy-taker, and then nip off home.

Tiger was the father-figure of the press box and, like Keith Miller, was loved by all. His colourful tales from press boxes and luncheon rooms around the country were always a feature. And those sitting closest were ever so privileged.

One day in Adelaide, at the back of the old wooden press box (which once caught fire after a Pommy scribe threw a still-lit Benson & Hedges between the floorboards), we made Tiger a life member of the Cricket Writers' Association and presented him with a small attaché case. The great man was genuinely humbled and thankful. He smiled broadly and expressed his gratitude. He knew he was amongst mates.

One afternoon in Brisbane, it rained so heavily that it seemed unlikely they'd be able to play for a month, let alone the next day. Deadlines met, we assembled in the downstairs bar at the Queensland Cricketers' Club. What started as a small shout gradually expanded. Tiger, who had been there from the start, looked around at what was now a huge circle. 'Is it mine?' he asked. 'How many is it? Twenty-four?'

Years later, while researching *Cricket's Colosseum: 125 Years of Test Cricket at the MCG*, I visited another legend, Billy Brown, in Brisbane. Even into his nineties, Bill was sharp, witty and, like the one and only Tiger, a fount of knowledge and anecdote. He, too, was in tip-top form. 'You'd better come up more often, Ken,' he quipped. 'We never usually get a spread like this.'

Laid out for us was a large plate of freshly made chicken-and-avocado sandwiches, a roly-poly cake and a large pot of fresh tea, expertly prepared by Bill's lovely wife, Barbara. Seeing me juggling a cuppa in one hand

and a plate in the other, Bill jumped up and lifted an extra chair across the room.

'I could have done that, Bill.'

'Oh no, Ken, you're the guest.'

When I rang the next day to thank him for his kindness, he said, 'Ken Piesse? There was someone here yesterday impersonating you . . . Oh Ken, it's you!'

During the same trip, I visited Sam Loxton, another of Don Bradman's Invincibles and one of my old coaches at Prahran Cricket Club. Sam was losing his sight and could read only with the help of an enlarger. But his stories and delivery were as sharp as ever. He told of a letter from a long-retired Don Bradman, imploring him to pick a young David Hookes for the Centenary Test. Hookes played.

Another postwar hero, Doug Ring, was stung by a bee on his spinning finger while opening his front gate on the eve of his maiden Test. The finger soon blew up to twice its normal size. Ring didn't know if he'd ever be chosen for his country again so he played, took six wickets and was selected on the '48 tour, the most famous of all. I carefully transcribed and stored all these stories, which were like manna from heaven for me.

Bill Ponsford told how he'd first lobbed at St Kilda and been selected as a 15-year-old in short pants. 'I couldn't hit it off the square much then,' he laughed, leaving it unsaid that it had taken them almost an hour to get him out. Years later, I found out I'd only been granted an audience thanks to a kindly word from Bodyline batsman Leo O'Brien. Leo was one of Ponny's oldest mates, and his toothy smile and engaging manner never changed. (He had played against the 'Big Ship', Warwick Armstrong. If Armstrong happened to overpitch one of his leg-breaks, he'd exclaim, 'Hit it!', coaching the kids while he was playing.)

A young Keith 'Nugget' Miller was one of many besotted by Ponsford and his record-breaking ways. He'd camp outside Ponsford's house in Orrong Road, Elsternwick, hoping the great man would emerge and sign an autograph. He never did. Even into his eighties and anxious for his own anonymity, Nugget still held court with those he trusted. Like the others, he was one of the greats of the game, and one of the many inspirations behind this book.

In recounting these tall stories and true, I'd like particularly to thank several of my colleagues. Robert Coleman's interviews for his admirable Victorian cricket history, *Seasons in the Sun*, reminded me of the humour of dearly departed trio Lindsay Hassett, Ernie McCormick and Harry 'Bull' Alexander; Mark Browning's lovingly researched 'Memory Lane' interviews from the old *Cricketer* magazine embellished my knowledge; and many others answered queries – from statisticians like Ross Dundas and Simon Fiedler to friends and relatives like Stan Gilchrist (Adam's dad).

I'm always keen to hear other anecdotes or records. For example, if you know of an opening stand to rival Keith Savage's (see QUADRUPLE CENTURION, page 163), please let me know. I can be contacted via my web site (see page i).

Almost all these anecdotes are from my one-on-one interviews during thirty years of writing about the greatest game of all. May you get as much enjoyment and entertainment from reading them as I did in their recounting.

ABC OF CRICKET

a is for Arm ball – the off-spinner's specialty, the one that spears away from the right-handers.

b is for Bunsen – a Bunsen burner, a raging turner (Old Trafford in '56, Chennai in 2004 and, in the old days, Sydney).

c is for Chin as in 'chin music' – short balls directed at the head.

d is for Doosra – Muthiah Muralidaran's special, the leg-break bowled with an off-spinning action.

e is for Extras or sundries – including penalty runs when the ball hits a helmet.

f is for Ferret – he comes in after the rabbits, and never higher than No. 11.

g is for a Golden – a golden duck, a first-baller, every batsman's nightmare.

h is for Happy hour – the last ten overs of a 50-over game.

i is for India's Irfan Pathan – the best young all-rounder in the world.

j is for Jaffa – the perfect delivery, unplayable.

k is for King pair – a first-baller in both digs.

l is for Long hop – a short ball, easily hit to the boundary.

m is for Mollydooker – a left-hander.

n is for Nude as in bowling 'nudies' (Mark Waugh specials) – nothing on 'em.

o is for Outriders – athletic types who ride the boundaries and like showing off their big arms.

p is for Poles as in 'hitting the poles' (wickets).

q is for Queensland, the long-time champions of Australian cricket, both at four-day and one-day level.

r is for Rabbit – one of the bottom three, as in king, queen, jack.

s is for Slider – Shane Warne's front-of-the-hand quicker one that, over the years, has trapped dozens lbw.

t is for Tom Nix – a six.

u is for Umbrella field – an arc of catchers behind the wicket.

v is for Victoria – the Bushrangers, the 2003–04 Pura Cup champions.

w is for *Wisden* – the game's long-running almanack, first published in 1864.

X is for Xavier Tras – Jim Maxwell's favourite term for sundries.

Y is for Yorker – the pace bowlers' special, one that is hard to combat, especially if it also reverses back at speed.

Z is for Zoota – one of many in the armoury of record-breaker Shane Warne.

ABILITY PLUS

It was towards the end of one Richmond nets session when former Test left-hander Leo O'Brien noticed the tall, sandy-headed kid bowling wrist-spin in the far net. It was Bradman Invincible-to-be Doug Ring, from Melbourne High.

'You spin it as well as bowl fast?' O'Brien asked.

'Oh yes,' said Ring. 'I try both.'

'Well, come and bowl to me in the first net – and bowl spin.'

Within a few deliveries, Ring bowled O'Brien with a sliding leg-break. Within a month, he was in Richmond's No. 1 side, as its specialist spinner – a Test career in the making.

AGE IS JUST A NUMBER (I)

From living out of a suitcase at a Hobart hotel to being a member of the most illustrious Test team of them all, Colin Miller's cricketing renaissance was one of the most extraordinary success stories, as Australia won 16 Tests in a row (1999–2001).

A genuine two-in-one bowler in the mould of a Bill Johnston, Miller first represented Australia at the age of 34, and enjoyed some magical and colourful times. He was noted just as much for his ever-changing hair colour as his ability to swerve and spin the ball from his baseballer's grip.

Had the mature-aged Miller realised just how dramatically his life was to change when he first started experimenting with off-breaks, he would have slowed down years earlier. In Adelaide (2000–01) he confirmed his status as Australia's No. 1 finger spinner, with man-of-the-match honours in Australia's thirteenth consecutive Test win. A journeyman who seemed destined to play only at state level before being included in the Australian touring team to Pakistan in 1998, Melbourne-born Miller would, he said, have retired years previously, had he not added off-spin to his repertoire.

Playing his first Boxing Day Test (2000) in front of his family and many of his old mates from Melbourne's west was a fairytale made even more memorable by his four wickets and two sixes – including one that soared over long-on, well past the ropes now common to all perimeters. 'Like Steve Waugh says, age is just a number,' he said.

AGE IS JUST A NUMBER (II)

Six for 6, including a double hat-trick and 18 opening up. It's a fair day's work, especially if you happen to be 61 years of age like Baxter farmer Tommy Deane. His big day out occurred in 1932–33 in the Northern Peninsula (now Mornington Peninsula) Association.

AGE IS JUST A NUMBER (III)

Chatty Victorian wicketkeeper Ray 'Slug' Jordon lied about his age, saying he was two years younger than he really was, when he first made the state squad in the late fifties. And he punched his captain, Bill Lawry, after he'd been dropped for the last time, in 1971.

'It was at the end of a social function and I was really dark when I found out about being sacked, because no one had bothered to ring to tell me,' Jordon said. 'I asked Phanto [Bill Lawry] why he hadn't shown me the decency of a phone call, given that we'd played 10 years together. He replied, "I never rang you when you were picked." So I smacked him one.'

SEE: TAKING A CHANCE (I), PAGE 199

ALL OUT FOR NONE

In 1933–34, Spring Creek was dismissed for none by Headingley Hill in the Allora and District Association in country Queensland. John Taylor took six for 0 and his brother William took three for 0.

ALL OUT FOR ONE

Sydney's Barker College Under 13s made just one against Waverley College (November, 1993), the solitary run being a leg bye. Seven of Tim Hume's eight victims were bowled and the interschool game was over in just 30 minutes.

'I was just bowling straight,' said Hume. 'I thought they were saving their best batsmen until last.'

SCOREBOARD

Barker College Under 13Bs
v. Waverley College Under 13Bs

Barker College		
Brommell	b. Hume	0
Toy	b. Hume	0
Wright	b. Hume	0
Hill	c. & b. Guttman	0

continued over page

5

Partridge	b. Hume	0
Ward	b. Hume	0
Factor	b. Guttman	0
Mallam	c. Scott, b. Hume	0
Tomlins	b. Hume	0
Sherlock	b. Hume	0
Rogers	not out	0
Extras		1
Total		1
Bowling: Guttman 4.2-4-0-2, Hume 4-4-0-8		

AN ALL-TIME PRIVILEGE

Among Gary Cosier's few regrets in cricket was to fail twice in the classic Centenary Test (Melbourne, 1977). However, he still had an important role to play, taking crucial short-leg catches to dismiss both Derek Randall and England's captain, Tony Greig, on the final afternoon.

'There had been a couple [of half-chances] earlier in the match I thought I could have got to, and Greg [Chappell, Australia's captain] did too,' said Cosier. 'I was really disappointed with the way I'd batted. Watching the highlights at the hotel one night, I saw a catch I should have got to, only to come up a few inches short. My first movement hadn't been towards the batsman.

'I resolved that night that I had to go forward and just go for it, no matter what. The tour of England was coming up after the match. I'd had such a rotten game. If I got hit, I got hit. It didn't matter. Even if it was only a half-chance which came my way, I just had to make it.

'Skully [Kerry O'Keeffe] was bowling and there was a half-chance from Derek Randall and I dived onto the wicket and just got there. I got lucky on that one.'

Cosier went on to tour England, and also went to the West Indies, before returning to Melbourne, where he continued to be a formidable player well into his thirties.

ALMOST A YANKEE

So powerful was Norman O'Neill's arm that the athletic Sydney superstar was offered a trial at spring training for the New York Yankees. The terms were lucrative, too: the equivalent of £2000 to sign, plus return airfares. Then 20, O'Neill had represented NSW at both cricket and baseball. In 1956, he was also selected for the Australian baseball team, only to be told he was ineligible for the Olympics as he could no longer be considered an amateur.

'I'd played a year of Sheffield Shield and accepted money, and in those days you had to be strictly amateur,' he said.

He was in the middle of an Ashes summer when the offer to play baseball for a living was made via visiting American Davis Cup coach Bill Talbert. While he rejected it – not wanting his cricket to be affected – he continued to play baseball for several more years, believing the skills of the game complemented his cricket and especially his work in the field, which was superlative.

ARCHER'S LUCKY BREAK

It's every budding Australian cricketer's ambition to be selected for an Ashes tour. Ron Archer had only just left Brisbane's Church of England Grammar School when his name was announced among Australia's '53 Ashes squad.

For the 19-year-old all-rounder, it was the culmination of all his dreams and a moment to savour. But he still remembers his embarrassment that his new ball-partner in the Test they were playing at the time (v. South Africa in Melbourne), South Australia's yorker specialist Geff Noblet, wasn't among the chosen ones.

'Nobby was a better bowler than I at that stage of our

careers,' Archer said. 'I could bat a bit, but I knew I'd been picked on potential [rather than performance].'

The tall Queenslander had played only nine first-class games, including a match for the Australian XI – an indication that Don Bradman and his fellow selectors rated his emerging abilities highly.

'I knew I was in their thoughts. I'd made a big score [for Queensland] against the South Africans that year and there was talk that I'd be picked. But you're never sure.

'At the time, though, I was getting cricketed out a bit. I was playing nearly every day and wasn't nearly as excited as I probably should have been.'

Also named in the squad was New South Wales teenager Ian Craig who, at 17 years and 239 days, remains the youngest ever recipient of a baggy green cap. He, too, had been playing state cricket for less than a year and was to cement his place for England with 53 and 47 on debut.

'It was very much a youth policy in those days,' said Archer. 'Things have changed now with professionalism, of course. Australia had a lot of success in picking young fellows ahead of more experienced and, at the time, better players. But Don Bradman, Stan McCabe, Richie Benaud, Alan Davidson and myself, to a degree, emerged from that youth policy . . . They were all pretty successful cricketers.'

ARISE, SIR RODNEY

When Rodney Hogg made his first truly important representative side, the Victorian Under 14s for the 1965 Schoolboys' Carnival in Brisbane, he was an opening batsman – and proud of it. Scores of 30, 16 and 0, however, severely dented his ego and never again was he to bat so high in the order. After one Test match failure, when he backed away and was bowled, he rang his wife and told her to erase the video tape immediately!

He is proud, however, of his career-best 52 against the West Indies at Bourda, then the highest Test score ever by an Australian No. 11. Hogg shared a 97-run stand in two-and-a-half hours with Tom Hogan, against a West Indian attack headed by the intimidating Joel Garner.

All of Hogg's other signature moments in Test cricket were to revolve around bowling, with Christmas 1978 being particularly sweet.

'If you're a Vic., the MCG is everything,' Hogg said. 'To have such a good game there was a career highlight. I wasn't back here [in Melbourne] to stick it up any Victorian selectors. I'd been given plenty of opportunities, including four second XI games, and simply hadn't got it together . . . When you make a change and go somewhere else, it stirs you a little bit.'

In a stunning series debut, Hogg was to claim 41 wickets at 12.75, including hauls of five for 30 and five for 36 at the MCG. A week later in Sydney, a banner on The Hill proclaimed him 'Sir Rodney Hogg'. Rarely had a fast bowler south of the divide earned such an accolade.

SEE: BAKED BEANS KING, PAGE 14

AN AUDIENCE WITH ROYALTY

For Melbourne *Herald* journalist Graham Eccles it was an audience with royalty – the interview of his life. Don Bradman was chairman of the Australian Cricket Board as well as a national selector and, during the rain-ruined Christmas Test in Melbourne in 1970–71, he told Eccles he simply wouldn't be interviewed. Refusing to take no for an answer, Eccles waited a few hours and rang again, this time speaking with Jessie Bradman who promised that Don, or she, would ring back. Eccles had to fill his page-two feature, 'On the Spot', for the next day, and Bradman was his last hope.

About 8 a.m. the following day, Eccles and photographer Ken Rainsbury went to Bradman's hotel and rang his room from the downstairs lobby. Bradman answered, again said no, and that he didn't have anything to say, anyway. Eccles assured him he did, and reminded him that Melbourne was his favourite city and the MCG his ultimate wicket. He also explained that he (Eccles) was up against it timewise and had nothing on stand-by to fill the space. He'd be most appreciative if he could chat . . .

There was a pause, and then, 'Oh, all right, come up.'

Eccles and Rainsbury hopped into the lift and knocked gingerly on the door. Bradman answered, saying, 'Hello Graham. Do you mind if I finish my prunes?'

'He got back on his bed, finished his breakfast and away we went,' said Eccles. 'It was just the easiest interview I'd conducted in 40 years. He was forthright and answered everything. He was great. It was so intimate I couldn't believe it. I just felt like I was a member of the family, sitting on the end of the bed; it was like coming in and having a chat with your parents.'

Forty minutes later, Eccles had his story and, back at the *Herald* office, was typing up slip after slip, with the editor taking each one as he finished it.

'It was the biggest thing we'd done in ages,' said Eccles. 'We'd got the Don!'

'AUNT, WHAT AUNT?'

Don Blackie was a legend at St Kilda, taking hundreds of wickets and, along with spinning cohort Bert Ironmonger, helping the Saints to an unprecedented four premierships in a row during the 1920s.

Playing against Blackie for the first time, Richmond's No. 11, Ernie McCormick, was met mid-pitch by the wily old champion on his way in to bat.

'Bad luck about your aunt . . .' Don said to McCormick.

'What aunt?'

'Tragedy,' said Don, shaking his head. 'Terrible experience. Give the folks my kindest regards.'

McCormick was still pondering the relation he didn't know he'd lost when struck in front by Blackie's slider, giving the veteran yet another five-wicket haul.

'Gave you the one about your aunt, did he?' St Kilda skipper and wicketkeeper Stuart King asked McCormick, as the players were walking off.

AUSTRALIA'S W. G.

George Giffen was an all-round cricketing colossus, Australia's version of England's cricket legend W. G. Grace. Giffen opened the South Australian batting *and* bowling in the 1880s and 1890s. Once, when asked if he thought there should be a change in the bowling, he said, 'Good idea, I'll go on at the other end!'

AWESOME

Sadanand Viswanath, India's 'keeper of the eighties, isn't exactly a household name in world cricket – except, that is, in the eyes of former Australian spin bowler Ray Bright. In a tour match in Bangalore in 1986–87, Viswanath struck Bright over the scoreboard and out of the ground, the biggest six Bright ever conceded.

'It was a monster,' Bright said. 'You can't hit a one wood that far. Initially I said, "Catch it!", before realising just how far it was going. The only bloke who could have caught it was the railway conductor half a block away. The boys just pissed themselves laughing. They couldn't believe how far it went. It was awesome. The biggest ever – off me, anyway.'

b

||||||||||||

BACK WITH THE KIDS

Genial Barry Jarman ranked a season with the Kensington Under 16s as one of his special thrills in cricket – and he was 42 at the time. Jarman made a comeback to play in a winning grand-final side with the Kensington kids in 1978–79. The former Test captain and 'keeper said his desire to see more boys continue to play throughout their teen years was the catalyst for his return.

'Many of the Adelaide schools no longer had cricket on their curriculums, and the clubs were finding a shortage of younger players flowing through into the system,' he said.

'The Adelaide Turf Cricket Association had an Under 16 and an Under 14 competition, and it was decided that so should the SACA [South Australian Cricket Association]. Rowe & Jarman sponsored it and many older players like myself got involved.

'It meant that I was a virtual captain–coach of the juniors. You weren't allowed to bat before No. 8 and had to retire at 20, and so on. It was just great being out there with the kids. It had a terrific impact on them and we had a ball ourselves.

'We played in a grand final and beat Glenelg. Ross Daniel was their captain and his side included a young Stephen Kernahan, who opened the bowling, and his mate [and fellow football star-to-be], Chris McDermott, who was 'keeper. Steve's dad, Harry [also a notable footballer], was coach and scorer.'

Jarman also filled in from A-grade through to C-grade at Kensington. He said it was very satisfying to play, several years later, with seven of the Under 16 premiership team in a match against his original club, Woodville. He believes the youth of today are tomorrow's cricketing leaders and need to be encouraged, even if one is too sore to walk the next day!

A BADGE OF HONOUR

During the Gilchrist family's annual Christmas shop one year in Shepparton in country Victoria, Adam, then 12, was walking past Kmart's front window. He spotted a pair of green-and-white wicketkeeping gloves that he just had to have. So proud was he of those gloves that he'd wear them around the house, including at the breakfast table while eating his Weet-Bix!

Even a broken nose while keeping wickets at primary school failed to blunt Adam's enthusiasm. His parents claim that he wore the bruise like a badge of honour – especially after being told that his hero, Rod Marsh, had suffered a similar injury when he first started wicketkeeping.

BAKED BEANS KING

Rodney Hogg was so determined to avoid food poisoning, as he embarked on his first tour of India in 1979, that he packed his own personal 'battle rations' – a dozen cans of Heinz baked beans. Hardly eating anything else, he duly started the series with 21 no-balls in the first Test and 21 more in the second – the worst overstepping problem by any Australian fast bowler on tour for more than 40 years.

'Haven't had a can since,' he says with a smile.

SEE: MADDER THAN MOST, PAGE 125

THE BALL OF HIS LIFE

George Tribe is in his eighties now, but still remembers one delivery, at practice almost 60 years ago, as the ball of his life.

'We were warming up for the Test match in Brisbane and Don Bradman came in for a hit,' said Tribe. 'All the photographers had followed us into the nets – after all, this was his first Test match in Australia for 10 years – and the very first ball I bowled went straight through him and hit his stumps. I couldn't believe it. He just straightened the stumps and threw the ball back. Then he started batting on his off-stump. He wanted to make certain that if he missed it again, it would hit his legs. He wasn't going to be bowled out again.'

Tribe, incidentally, had originally been an orthodox finger-spinner, before switching to wrist-spin. He reckoned that with the change in the lbw law (1935), he had greater opportunities for taking wickets with wrist-spin, even with the ball pitching outside a right-hander's off stump.

'Prior to the rule change, you had to pitch between the wickets and, as my finger-spinner was spinning away from the right-handers, I reckoned I could take more wickets spinning it back in,' he said.

One day, while playing in sub-district ranks at Brighton, he was bowling orthodox spin from the southern end when their fast bowler, a left-hander, hit him for a huge six. It went right out of the ground, bounced once on Beach Road and disappeared over the wall on to the sand.

'I said to our captain as they were retrieving the ball that I might as well have a go with my wrist-spinners. I finished up getting seven wickets from the other end and that was the start of it all.'

SEE: HUMMING 'EM DOWN, PAGE 102

BALLARAT BOYS

Cricket at the Eastern Oval in Ballarat pre-dates the Eureka rebellion. The heritage-listed main grandstand is 100 years old and has hosted many of the world's best, from famed Englishmen W. G. Grace, Jack Hobbs and Herbert Sutcliffe to the immortal Victor Trumper and, more recently, fabled Sri Lankans Sanath Jayasuriya, Aravinda de Silva and Arjuna Ranatunga.

Cricket was first played there on Boxing Day, 1853, at the height of gold fever, when a pick-up match was contested between the Canadian and the Gravel Pit diggers.

Cricket historian Lloyd Jenkins says H. H. Stephenson's 1862 touring English team, the first to Australian shores, also played at the Eastern. And the tradition continued until recently, with almost all the major touring teams scheduling a game at Ballarat's sporting showpiece. At the first 'Great International', it cost two shillings and sixpence for admission and five shillings to sit in the grandstand.

The legendary Dr Grace played at the ground several times, including the 1891–92 match when he top-scored with 62 and Twenty of Ballarat was beaten by an innings and 134 runs. Results against the odds were common. In this game, visiting fast bowlers John Sharpe and Johnny Briggs produced match figures of twelve for 28 and ten for 53 respectively.

One of the Eastern's greatest days occurred in 1992, when more than 13 000 attended Match 12 of the World Cup between England and Sri Lanka. Rex Hollioake, then the president of the Ballarat Cricket Association, said dozens of fans waited all night in order to be first through the gates the next morning to secure the best seats for the match.

'We had to close the gates at 10 a.m. Hundreds couldn't get in,' he said. 'We had WIN Television [regional channel] there and it ended up going to millions all around the world.'

Jack Hill and Percy Beames remain the best-known of those Ballarat 'Old Boys' who came and conquered in the big smoke. Hill, known as 'Snarler' for his ferocious appeals, attended St Pat's College in Ballarat before coming to Melbourne and playing for St Kilda. He represented Australia on the 1953 tour of England and the 1955 tour of the West Indies.

Beames went on to captain Victoria at cricket and football, and worked for years as the chief cricket and football writer for *The Age* newspaper. Once, he all but hit the clock in the old members' stand at the MCG. But for the War, he almost certainly would have played for Australia. His nephew, David, opened the bowling with North Melbourne in the late seventies.

Others to do themselves proud in the city include Bungaree's Damien Ryan, who once threw a ball 113 yards and two feet at a long-throwing contest at the

AN ALL-STAR BALLARAT XII

1. Ron Furlong
2. Pon Beames
3. Peter Oxlade
4. Keith Rawle (c)
5. John Hollioake
6. Damien Ryan
7. Arthur Meiklejohn
8. Ron Plover (w/k)
9. Shane Harwood
10. Rex Hollioake
11. Jack Hill
12. David Beames

Centenary Test. He played in a premiership at Footscray and continues to coach juniors. Ron Furling opened for Victoria against the West Indian express Wes Hall, while gifted footballer–cricketer Keith Rawle and expressman Hollioake had many great moments against touring teams.

SEE: STREETS AHEAD, PAGE 194

BATTING BUNNIES

Bob Holland, the only Australian to make five consecutive Test ducks, is still a fixture in the Newcastle second XI club ranks, batting only when he has to and never higher than No. 11. His infamous run of Test 'globes' came in 1985, when he was in his fortieth year and batting well and truly from memory.

'It got to a stage where I wasn't even game to try and hit the ball,' Holland said. 'I was scared I was going to get another one.

'We played in Perth and [New Zealand's] Richard Hadlee was bowling. Just about every fielder was behind the wicket. I pushed at it and got it high up on the splice and it only just cleared the guy in at short cover and I got a run [his first in 105 days]. By that stage, it was almost as good as taking a wicket!'

Ranking with other notable No. 11s Stuart MacGill, Alan Hurst, Jim Higgs and Bert 'Dainty' Ironmonger as the ultimate bunnies, Holland had occasionally opened in his younger days in Newcastle. But, he said, the runs began to dry up once he started in Sheffield Shield ranks with NSW.

MacGill's double-figure scores were also rare, other than one innings of 43 during an Ashes Test in Melbourne in 1998–99 (when he all but outscored centurion Steve Waugh), and one tenth-wicket stand of 219 with NSW's

Dominic Thornely, in 2004–05 against Western Australia in Sydney. (MacGill's share here was 27!) Hurst made a record six ducks in a series in 1978–79, while Higgs was bowled by the only delivery he faced on the '75 Ashes tour. The daddy of them all, however, was Ironmonger (career average 2.62). He was so inept that even Dolly – the horse responsible for rolling the MCG wicket – would get animated at the sight of Bert in pads, realising she would soon be needed! Ironmonger's wife once rang the MCG rooms to be told that Bert had just gone out to bat. 'That's okay,' she said, 'I'll hang on.'

The most bowled batsman in Australian Test history – on a percentage scale – is Queensland's perennial No. 11, Carl Rackemann, who was bowled nine times out of 10. Using his pads as a first line of defence, 'Big Mocca' once took 73 minutes to get off the mark (v. England, Sydney, 1990–91), before 'racing' to nine in 107 minutes!

LOWEST TEST BATTING AVERAGES

Batsman	Tests	Average
Jack Saunders	14	2.2
Bert Ironmonger	14	2.6
Bob Holland	11	3.1
Ernie Jones	19	5.0
Jim Higgs	22	5.6
Alan Hurst	12	6.0

Note: Australians only; 10 Tests minimum

SEE: WHIT'S BIG MOMENT, PAGE 224

BETTER THAN THE DON

Only one man topped Sir Donald Bradman's Sheffield Shield batting average of 109.8: Dr Harry Owen Rock who, in just four Shield games, averaged 112 – including a century on debut (Sydney, 1924). Dr Rock's commitment to medicine saw him practise in Newcastle for 30 years.

BETTING AGAINST THE BOY

No wonder Glenn McGrath was cock-a-hoop when he scored a personal best of 61 in the Brisbane Test of 2004–05. After years of sniggering about the big fella's batting ability, Shane Warne and Mark Waugh each had to cough up $1000, having bet against McGrath ever making a Test 50.

BIG BERTHA

One of the secrets behind Bill Ponsford's record-breaking ways was his choice of bats. When most players used bats weighing no more than 2 lb 3 oz, Ponny's was closer to 2 lb 10 oz. He could pierce the in-field even with a defensive push.

So famous was Ponsford's bat that it was given a nickname: 'Big Bertha'. And so often did Ponny find Big Bertha's middle that, once, the bat was measured and found to be ever so slightly wider than allowed.

'Ponny was a great player in every respect and a great accumulator of runs,' Don Bradman told Melbourne writer Robert Coleman. 'He didn't appear to be smashing the bowling to pieces all the time, but nevertheless the runs accumulated and, before you knew where you were, you'd find 50 on the board and then 100. He always gave the impression that he had a very, very broad bat. Clarrie Grimmett reckoned he'd rather bowl to anybody except Ponsford. He reckoned he was the hardest man to get out.'

His long-time opening partner, Bill Woodfull, said Ponny was the greatest batsman he ever saw against slow bowlers. 'He was murder on them,' he said.

Incidentally, the bat with which Ponny made his epic farewell 266 at the Oval in 1934, a Spalding W. H. Ponsford Autograph, remains in the Ponsford family – still with its three pieces of sticking plaster and autographs of each of the players from the competing teams. It is a priceless example of early Australian cricket memorabilia, along with Bradman's 1948 Test cap and the Don's record-high 334 Test bat.

SEE: AN OLD FAVOURITE, PAGE 143

THE BIGGEST STEAL OF ALL

For the ecstatic Australians, Christmas had come early, and they sang and resang 'Under the Southern Cross I Stand'. Set 181 to win at the Sinhalese Sports Club, Sri Lanka had tumbled from 2/127 to 164 all out, to lose the first Test of 1992–93 by 16 runs. The Sri Lankans retreated into a small backroom to escape the singing, but still they could hear it. No one said a word.

'It was like a funeral house,' said senior player Roshan Mahanama. 'It was like someone close to each and every one of us had died. There could not have been a more disappointing loss. We had dominated for four days and two sessions, only to fall at the last hurdle. It remains my blackest moment in cricket, my darkest day.'

The twin destroyers were Greg Matthews with four for 76 and Shane Warne with three for 11, including his final spell of three for none. It had taken the Melbourne youngster the entire match to find a good length and he spun the ball sharply, ripping through the bottom order and revitalising his career. The Australians were as astonished as the Sri Lankans were bewildered. It had been the biggest steal of all.

BILLYGOAT GRUFF

What happens on tour stays on tour (or so it's said). But when a fully grown billygoat is smuggled into someone's room, it's hard to stay mum.

The '38 Australians were in between Tests at a small village outside Manchester, staying in a large country house. Fun-loving pair Lindsay Hassett and Merv Waite were kicking on late one night when they heard a bleat. Going outside to investigate, they came across a billygoat on the side of a small hill near a summerhouse.

Sufficiently lubricated, the boys thought they'd try to catch the goat. Several rugby tackles later, however, neither had anything to show for their efforts except a badly soiled suit.

Knowing his mate liked to yak – and not wanting those back home in Geelong to hear of the time he'd been outsmarted by a goat – Hassett went inside. Grabbing a tin of broken biscuits from the kitchen, he laid an enticingly sweet trail from the hill down to the summerhouse. The goat obligingly ate each biscuit in turn, edging closer and closer to his captors before finally succumbing to a headlock.

Delighted to have made the capture at last, Hassett and Waite nudged their prize upstairs to the Australian team's sleeping quarters. They quietly opened the door to Tiger O'Reilly and Stan McCabe's room and pushed their new friend in before shutting the door again. They returned to their own room, just around the corner, and listened with their door ajar. For about 30 seconds, all was quiet, before the goat let go a tremendous bleat.

'What in the bloody hell was that, Stan?' said O'Reilly, closest to the door.

'Dunno. Might have been a tortoise . . .'

'Tortoise be buggered,' said O'Reilly, turning on the light and confronting the goat.

With a thump and a body slam, Billy was soon out of there. Hassett and Waite suppressed their laughter and avoided detection by quickly shutting their own door.

Next morning at breakfast, Hassett innocently asked O'Reilly, 'Sleep well, Tige?'

Without bothering to look up, O'Reilly said, 'So, it was you, you little bugger!'

SEE: LOVABLE LINDSAY, PAGE 123

BIRTHDAY BLISS

In a lifetime of cricket, record-breaker Shane Warne has only ever taken one hat-trick. It happened in front of almost 10 000 Ashes devotees in the Christmas Test of 1994–95 in his home town, Melbourne. David Boon was on the end of it – a half-chance from England No. 10, Devon Malcolm.

'In that instance, everyone is basically saying I hope he doesn't hit it to me as I don't want to stuff it up,' said Boon. 'But it happened to come my way. Luckily, it was one of those ballooned ones to bat-pad . . . I had to make a yard [throwing himself to his right] and, thankfully, it stuck [in his outstretched right hand]. It was my birthday that day and a lovely present to put beside the cake.'

A BIT ONE-SIDED

Few backyard Test matches have been as furiously contested as those between the two Lee brothers, Shane and Brett. One of their rituals was to hose down the driveway so the ball would skid on more. And attaching electrical tape to half the tennis ball made it swing prodigiously.

When a ball went on to the roof and was caught in the guttering, rather than shimmy up a ladder to collect it, Shane would give Brett some money to cycle down to the shops in Oak Flats and buy more. Clearing out the gutters one day, Bob Lee, the boys' father, found almost 60 balls. 'He had a fair idea why the gutters were constantly overflowing,' said Brett.

The brothers had only just graduated from the taped tennis ball to a harder version when Shane struck Brett, three years his junior, flush on the throat, triggering a premature break in play.

An even bigger sting, however, was the time Shane made 256, despite numerous appeals, keeping young Brett out in the hot sun most of the afternoon. When Brett was finally allowed a hit, he nicked the first ball and his brother immediately walked inside. Game over!

'I started crying and Mum came out and made him go back and bowl to me again,' said Brett. 'He got me [again] two or three balls later. It was a bit one-sided.'

SEE: BROTHERLY LOVE, PAGE 35

BOOK LAUNCHES WITH A DIFFERENCE

Dougie Walters so loved the Sydney Cricket Ground Hill and all its patrons that he launched the second of his autobiographies there (1981). Homemade 'DOUG WALTERS STAND' banners adorned the surrounds and guests were invited to dress in thongs and shorts, and enjoy standard Hill fare: pies washed down by a Tooheys or two. 'I wouldn't have had it any other way,' said Doug.

Victorian legend Merv Hughes launched his book, *My Life And Other Funny Stories*, at Pentridge Prison, where Ronald Ryan, the last man to be hanged in Victoria, died in 1967. Like Doug's, his book sold in the tens of thousands.

BOSOM BUDDIES

Ray Lindwall and Keith Miller were the closest of buddies, and Lindwall always marvelled at his mate's gift for remembering names.

'Even if he hadn't met people for years, he'd still know them next time he met them,' Lindwall told author Robert Coleman. 'He had a flair for knowing your name. I found out there was a little catch to it, though; after a few years, he used to call all his friends either 'Fatty' for the boys or 'Honey' for the girls. It was a trick he taught me but I didn't benefit from it very much!'

Lindwall said Miller was the life of the party on tour, and the pair would regularly have a few beers after dinner.

'Sometimes there's nothing else to do at night, and most of us would have anything from three to eight beers before bed. We could sleep in until about 8 or 9 a.m., so there was enough time to get plenty of sleep. And when you wake up, it only takes 10 minutes to run around a field and you're as fit as a fiddle again. Keith could do that just as well as anyone else, if not better.'

SEE: GEMS FROM NUGGET, PAGE 80

BOUQUETS FOR STRATTY

When whistlestop Gippsland town Stratford (population 1000) defeated Sale (population 17 000) for the 2002–03 premiership, the bouquets were well-deserved. Local newsagent Neil Tatterson top-scored with a ton.

'We were the minnows in that match and every time we beat them it's sweet,' said the diminuitive Tatterson.

Recruited from Kilmaney where he won four premierships, it was Tatterson's second flag at Stratford, where he has filled various roles, from president and treasurer to groundsman.

'It's all part of living in a country town. You get involved,' he said.

Tatterson, 40, figured in five Australian country carnivals and was an All-Australian in 1996.

BOY WONDER

Billy Wilson began his career on the harsh concrete wickets of Ouyen in the hot Victorian Mallee. As a teenager, representing Veterans against Ouyen, he top-scored with 11 and took all 10 wickets for 41, having taken seven for 7 in the previous round.

At Melbourne Country Week in 1933–34 and bowling left-arm chinamen like the great Chuck Fleetwood-Smith, he took 27 wickets. And in his first major game in Melbourne, for Colts against University, he captured six for 39 and four for 28.

Wilson was to represent Victoria, but he was a drifter and moved to Adelaide and then Sydney, leaving his early promise unfulfilled.

BRAD'S A BUSHIE AT HEART

At 36, Brad Glenn reckons it's only now that he's learning how to bat. Captain of Victoria for five Australian country-cricket carnivals, Glenn is one of the most high-profile players outside the Melbourne metropolitan area. Mixing his top-order batting with his wicketkeeping skills, he made Victoria's state squad in the early nineties.

Now captain–coach of Rosebud (on Melbourne's Mornington Peninsula), Glenn says the opportunity to play in national carnivals has been a huge bonus.

'I'd lost my state squad contract and felt I wasn't going to play for Victoria, so I left district cricket to play on the Peninsula, at first with Mt Eliza and, for the last three or four years, with Rosebud.

'In hindsight, I'm just learning to bat now. Despite what I once thought, I'm not a hard hitter and it suits me best to play more of a percentage game.'

In 2003–04 Glenn made four centuries, but his knees were so sore from almost 20 years of wicketkeeping that he withdrew from the national championships. 'I can run all day, but it's just the bending [that is a problem],' he said.

In his impressive city career, he played in a one-day premiership team at club level with legend Dean Jones. He also played in a flag team with Melbourne seconds alongside international-to-be Brad Williams.

There's a huge difference, he says, between playing on the MCG and on many of the bush grounds.

'One Christmas at Rosebud, I hit one through the covers and said, "That's four," and just stood there. But it hit a big patch of weed and in it stayed, [with] the bloke at third man running around to pick it up five or so yards inside the fence. If I felt like an idiot then, I felt like a bigger one in a match against Peninsula Old Boys soon afterwards. I hit one right off the middle and again said, "That's four," only for the bloke at gully to take a blinder [catch]. You don't reckon they got into me after that!'

BRADMAN BRIEFS

- As scorer for Bowral's first XI, young Don Bradman would always bring his whites along in case a team member failed to turn up. When someone was ill, he filled in and made 37 not out in his first game of open-age cricket.
- He was 12 when he first visited the Sydney Cricket Ground and saw Charlie Macartney, the 'Governor-General', make 170 against England. 'I shall never be satisfied,' vowed the young Don, 'until I play on this ground.'

- Having left school at 14, his first job was as a clerk for a real-estate company, Deer & Westbrook, in Bong Bong Street, Bowral.
- For two years, at the ages of 15 and 16, Bradman played more tennis than cricket and was a Country Week representative.
- He was just 17 when he made his first triple-century: 300 for Bowral v. Moss Vale for the Tom Mack Cup, with the final lasting five Saturdays.
- His NSW teammates nicknamed him 'Braddles' and, on tour, would ask him to play tunes on the piano.
- Having enjoyed a record-breaking first tour of England, Bradman recorded 'Old Fashioned Locket' and 'Our Bungalow of Dreams' (78 rpm) for Columbia Records.
- In his final innings at The Oval, in 1948, he was bowled for zero by an Eric Hollies googly. Minutes before, he'd been given three cheers by the English team, led by Norman Yardley, and the crowd had joined the players in singing 'For He's a Jolly Good Fellow'.
- Such was Bradman's astonishing success as a batsman that he was always expected to score a century. 'BRADMAN FAILS' was the banner headline one day in the *London Star*. He had made 80.
- Thirty-seven of the Don's 117 centuries were of 200-plus, including a highest at Test level of 334.
- As a single figures golfer, he regular beat his age at his home club in Adelaide, Kooyonga.
- In 1936, he rejected an offer of £3000 to write about the Ashes Tests rather than playing in them.
- With his occasional leg-spinners, he took two Test wickets: the West Indian Ivan Barrow, and England's batting great, Walter Hammond.
- As Australian captain, he averaged 101, compared with 98 as a player.
- Melbourne was his most successful Australian Test ground. He averaged 128 at the MCG in 11 Tests.

- Only 15 bowlers ever bowled him for a duck (Alec Bedser did it twice). In all matches against English attacks including Bedser, Bradman averaged 92.
- In all cricket, the Don made more than 50 000 runs at an average of 90, with 211 centuries.
- As an administrator on official South Australian Cricket Association committees from 1935–36 to 1985–86, he attended 1713 meetings.

SEE: DEVOTION AND DEDICATION, PAGE 57

BRADMAN OF THE BUSH

Of Henry Gunstone's eight premierships with St Andrews (just outside Melbourne), one has extra significance: the final in which he made a double-century, leaving the opposition so disgruntled they didn't even bother batting!

'I batted into a third day,' said Gunstone. 'Swifts had beaten us once before, earlier that summer [1977–78] at Stawell, and I didn't want to give them another chance.'

Not only did Gunstone, then aged 37, bat through the entire first two days, but through part of the third as well.

'We'd finished on top of the ladder and a draw was good enough for us to win the flag,' said Gunstone.

St Andrews made 6/406 declared, and with only four hours left on the final day, the Swifts' skipper conceded. Asked how the opposition felt, Gunstone said, 'They weren't too happy.'

Most bush grand finals now are played to at least a first innings' finish, even if it takes two full weekends to do it. Gunstone played in 14 grand finals with Aradale and St Andrews in Western Victoria, winning eight and losing six. He never tired of premiership success.

'Some people say that they [grand finals] are just another game, but they're not. You don't get to play in many,' he said. 'I was luckier than most and played in quite a few. Overall, you're doing a good job if you can win one in two.'

One particularly sweet flag for St Andrews came after three consecutive grand-final defeats at the hands of High School, whose team included a fast bowler from Melbourne called Russell Lewis.

'They'd kept beating us, but we won the fourth one and pretty easily, too,' said Gunstone. 'Russell was one of the best fast bowers in the country – brisk and a great competitor. We had many battles and probably finished pretty square. He'd always be coming at you. We would have liked him to play more often for Grampians [in Country Week]. Every time he played, he'd clean up the opposition.'

Scorer of 129 centuries, including one on his wedding day, Gunstone, now 65, was also a League footballer with South Melbourne and played district cricket in Melbourne before returning to the family's dairy farm in Ararat.

THE BRADMAN OF
CRICKET-BOOK COLLECTORS

At the height of the Brisbane floods in 1974, Pat Mullins, the Bradman of Australian cricket-book collectors, was asked by his children which book he'd try to save if the family house was endangered. 'You want the truth?' he said. 'I'd go down with 'em all!'

The son of a North Queensland publican, Mullins started collecting at the age of nine, when he bought the Herbert Sutcliffe batting and the M.S. Nicholls bowling flicker-books. After that, he began to collect clippings from the newspapers that his father, Pat snr, used to wrap bottles at the hotel. Pat jr kept scrapbooks into his late sixties, eventually having more than 300. Among his most prized was one once owned by Golden Age Test batsman Roger Hartigan.

An undistinguished player, Mullins did make the first XI at Mt Carmel College in Charters Towers for three years, from the age of 14. His passion for cricket and its literature was, however, boundless. The opportunity to meet a young Don Bradman in northern Queensland in 1931 further fueled his love of the game.

Mullins' library at his Coorparoo home featured ultra-wide shelving from floor to ceiling, with books double- and sometimes triple-stacked. A generous and welcoming friend, he shared his collection and cuttings with hundreds – including Sir Donald Bradman, who came to visit one day and stayed for tea.

A solicitor for more than 50 years, Mullins bought everything with a cricket mention and, along with well-known Sydney cricket writer Phil Derriman, co-authored several editions of the acclaimed anthology *Bat and Pad: Writings on Australian Cricket*, first published in 1984 and re-released in 2001. Many of the stories in one of my early cricket books, *The Great Australian Book of Cricket Stories* (1982) were gleaned from the Mullins collection.

BRADMAN'S LAST STAND

Having triumphed so often at the MCG, it was fitting that 40-year-old Don Bradman scored a farewell ton in his last appearance at the MCG during his own testimonial match in 1948–49.

After leading the team to England in 1948, the Don played only three further games the following Australian season: one at his favourite MCG, where he'd made nine centuries in 11 Tests; one in Sydney, where he was bounced by Keith Miller; and the other in his home town of Adelaide, for the benefit of one of South Australia's foremost past cricketers, Arthur Richardson.

Bradman's 123 in just two-and-a-half hours in Melbourne was to be his 117th and final major century

BRADMAN'S RECORD

Tests	Inns	NO	HS	Runs	Ave	100s
52	80	10	334	6996	99.94	29

Player: 1928–29 to 1948
Captain: 1936–37 to 1948

– and there was an element of controversy to it, when he was dropped at 97. Some among the crowd of 52 960 felt the fieldsman, Colin McCool, had deliberately grassed the catch. However, the bowler, Bill Johnston, said it was far from a 'gimme'.

'It was a real skyer and Col, who was at square leg, had to make ground to it and catch it over his shoulder.'

Did he mean to put it down?

'I don't know,' said Johnston. 'I never asked Col. Having dropped it, it landed on his toe and he kicked it over the boundary, Don going from 97 to 101!'

There was tumultuous cheering for both Bradman and McCool, a member of the Don's team to England the previous winter. Most felt McCool had made an admirable sporting gesture.

While Johnston was denied the Don's wicket on this memorable Saturday afternoon, he dismissed him in the second innings, caught behind for 10. And three months later in Adelaide, in Bradman's last match, he dismissed him again (for 30) – 'an inside edge into his stumps', Johnston remembers. 'It turned out to be his last innings. He injured an ankle and couldn't bat in the second innings.'

THE BRIEFEST OF NETS

Even by Doug Walters' considerable standards, this night on the town was an extremely late one. Returning to his Indian hotel room in the early hours of the morning, Walters came across a pile of loose bedposts in a corner. He reckoned they were ideal for a game of fiddlesticks. The noise reverberated up and down the corridors, waking most in the immediate vicinity.

At practice later that morning, Doug hit the first in the middle and walked straight out of the net. 'What are you doing, Doug?' asked his captain, Bill Lawry.

'I'm hitting 'em in the middle,' he said. 'You don't want me to waste those shots here, do you?'

Even Lawry had no answer to that.

BRIGHTLY FADES THE DON

It was the ultimate sporting fairytale: bush kid rises like a meteor, surpassing the feats of even the most celebrated. But could he still do it in his fortieth year? And on his farewell tour? Don Bradman soon provided the answers, with his triumphant team to England in 1948 becoming known as the Invincibles.

The Don hadn't intended that his team go unbeaten during their 34-match program; retaining the Ashes by playing aggressive, attractive cricket was his priority. He wanted to bring some joy back into the lives of those communities ravaged by World War II. As the tour progressed, however, and his team swept from success to success, it was soon obvious that they possessed awesome strength and were as powerful as any set of Aussie invaders. Leading into the first Test at Trent Bridge, the Australians had won 10 and drawn two of their first 12 games, and Bradman was keen to extend the winning run. He still had memories of The Oval in 1938, when

England batted three days for 900-plus.

Ray Lindwall and Keith Miller provided the launching pad and big Bill Johnston, coming on as first change bowler, finished it off. The English were bowled out for just 165 in the first innings. Captain Norman Yardley had elected to bat first but the wicket was fine; there were no excuses.

The Australians resumed on the Friday morning at 0/17, with the Test in the balance. Bradman regarded the first days of a new series as the most important. He wanted to make an immediate statement – and inspire others around him. Taking his place at his favourite No. 3 slot, he saw off the menacing Surrey off-spinner Jim Laker, who had taken three for 22 from his first 12.4 overs and, with his deputy Lindsay Hassett, shared a crucial century stand for the fifth wicket.

Bradman was unusually subdued and was even slow handclapped as he struggled, initially, to pierce Yardley's defensive field settings and leg-stump line. It took him three-and-a-half hours to reach 100 – his twenty-eighth Test century, and his eighteenth against England. It had been chanceless, though he'd very nearly played on to Alec Bedser's second ball. The Australians swept to an eight-wicket victory, immediately stamping their authority on the series.

At Headingley later that summer, in one of the most famous matches of all, Bradman made his twenty-ninth and final century as Australia chased 404 on the final day. They made the runs with seven wickets and 10 minutes to spare.

TRIBUTES

Bill Ponsford: *I knew it was always hopeless trying to chase Bradman. He was ruthless.*

P. F. 'Plum' Warner: *Don Bradman was so good he could have made a century in the dark.*

Bill Johnston, recalling the Don's influence on the '48 tourists: *We all had a great respect for him. He treated us as grown men and let us do our own thing. But he always wanted us to be fit!*

BROM'S ROCKET-ARM

Few had a more powerful throwing arm than 1934 Australian tourist Ernie Bromley. In a throwing contest at the MCG during the Bodyline summer, 'Brom' unleashed a 120-metre throw that, but for a safety net, would have soared into the crowd.

Of postwar Australians, only Norman O'Neill and perhaps a young Ricky Ponting could possibly have matched Bromley's arm. His low throws alone, which brought whistles of admiration and applause, were worth the cost of admission.

Bromley's arm was still strong even after a break from cricket during the War, and he continued his habit of pinging the ball in, even from close range. Once, in a club match for St Kilda, he conceded four overthrows and skipper Hec Oakley made him fetch the ball from the other side of the Junction Oval. Oakley was forever telling Brom to throw fast only when the run-out was possible!

Born in Western Australia, Bromley had 11 seasons with the Saints, his last at 36 years of age. He'd moved east to win first-class recognition, as WA was not part of the old Sheffield Shield competition until after World War II.

SEE: BALLARAT BOYS, PAGE 16

BROTHERLY LOVE

Scuffles were part and parcel of the Hussey brothers' backyard Tests at Mullaloo, a Perth seaside suburb.

David Hussey said there were few rules, except he'd always bat first.

'It was the only way I could get a bat,' he said. 'I could rarely get [brother] Michael out. A few times there – invariably after a fifty-fifty decision had gone against me – I'd refuse to bowl and either lock myself in the car or bedroom, or sprint down the beach. It got serious all right. Often. But we've matured a bit since then. We had to!'

BROTHERS WITH ARMS

Tommy Lloyd and younger brother Des have each played more than 500 games of bush cricket and are perhaps Victorian country cricket's most famous brothers. While Tommy is best known in the western districts, Des shifted to Ballarat where he still umpires.

Tommy amassed almost 1450 wickets in 518 games for Colac, including 50 or more in eight seasons. He also took hundreds more at Country Week and in representative games. A legendary figure at Ballarat Country Week, where he played 37 times, Tommy also appeared at Melbourne Country Week twelve times. In a grand final, playing for Colac against Coragulac, Tommy shared a 36-run last-wicket stand with Des (who was playing only his fourth game) to lift Colac to the title.

Born and bred in Colac, where their parents ran a dairy farm (with a concrete wicket down the side of the house), the Lloyds were guests of honour at Colac Cricket Club's 150th celebrations in 2005.

Once, in a XXXX promotional game in Warrnambool involving Victorians Ray Bright, Jamie Siddons and Tony Dodemaide, Tommy reckons he had Siddons caught behind, only for the umpire to rule against him.

'Afterwards, Ray wanted to know where I'd been as he reckoned I bowled a better line than [Test spinner]

Dutchy Holland,' Tommy said. 'And I was 50 at the time!'

Des was also noted for his longevity and was a fine all-rounder, with a career-best score of 229 and best analysis of eight for 22. He was 50 when he played in his last A-grade premiership, for Golden Point against Ballarat-Redan – and he took a couple of wickets with his offies, too.

Two years earlier, Des had played in another Golden Point premiership, in which he shared a match-sealing sixth-wicket stand of 130. A former captain of Golden Point, 'when I was a young bloke' (in his mid-thirties), Des amassed 7000 runs for the club at an average of 27, and took more than 450 wickets at an average or 17.

TOMMY LLOYD: COLAC'S BRADMAN OF SPIN

Season	Overs	Wkts	Ave	Flag	
1952–53	28	6	13.33	✓	(12th man)
1956–57	138	47	7.46	✓	
1957–58	171	37	10.08		
1958–59	173	33	11.03		
1959–60	197	30	16.96		
1960–61	192	47	10.72	✓	
1961–62	303	65	18.69		
1962–63	163	28	22.00		
1963–64	194	38	17.52		
1964–65	176	45	12.77		
1965–66	204	52	12.42		
1966–67	136	34	15.15		
1967–68	149	45	11.49	✓	
1968–69	174	47	10.44		
1969–70	167	47	11.30		
1970–71	149	36	14.19		
1971–72	168	61	7.95	✓	
1972–73	177	69	8.26		

continued over page

Season	Overs	Wkts	Ave	Flag
1973–74	203	54	12.18	
1974–75	194	63	9.42	✓
1975–76	160	50	10.84	✓
1976–77	189	51	12.19	
1977–78	169	29	17.10	✓
1978–79	176	35	12.82	
1979–80	125	24	13.33	
1980–81	139	34	11.55	
1981–82	147	24	19.33	
1982–83	137	26	9.77	✓
1983–84	187	39	11.20	
1984–85	188	38	13.60	
1985–86	184	39	13.51	
1986–87	85	10	24.50	
1987–88	120	14	26.14	
1988–89	134	16	21.50	
1989–90	118	24	13.12	
1990–91	105	14	20.00	
1991–92	124	19	15.42	
1992–93	70	13	12.38	
1993–94*	147	29	14.27	
1994–95*	160	29	15.62	
Total	6320	1441	16.00	

* playing down the grades (not in the first XI)

SEE: THE X-FACTOR, PAGE 229

C
|||||||||||

CALENDAR-YEAR KING

No one in Test history has surpassed the deeds of West Indian great Viv Richards during 1976. His scores are part of cricketing folklore.

VIV RICHARDS IN 1976

Match	Place	Scores
v. Australia	Sydney	44 & 2
v. Australia	Adelaide	30 & 101
v. Australia	Melbourne	50 & 98
v. India	Bridgetown	142
v. India	Port of Spain	130 & 20
v. India	Port of Spain	177 & 23
v. India	Kingston	64
v. England	Nottingham	232 & 63
v. England	Manchester	4 & 135
v. England	Leeds	66 & 38
v. England	The Oval	291
Total: 11 matches, 1710 runs, 90 average		

CAPTAIN GRUMPY

Few were as intense or as openly grumpy as Allan Border, Australia's stalwart captain of the eighties and early nineties.

It was the deciding Test on a steamy, early-summer day in Perth, and New Zealand was winning. Trying to be as helpful as possible during an interval, Australia's twelfth man, Ray Bright, offered Border a cool drink – only to be told what to do with it!

'It wasn't funny at the time, but it is now,' said Bright. 'He lived up to his nickname that day.'

During Border's final Test series, in South Africa in 1993–94, he was not out at one of the intervals and came in cursing, having struggled to hit the ball off the square. Ian Healy grabbed his bat and put it in a bucket of ice, 'just to cool it down, AB'. Border's reaction? Unprintable.

CARRYING HIS BAT AT LORD'S

Bill Brown loved Lord's, cricket's holy of holies. Given half a chance, he says he would have carried the Lord's wicket all over England, so blessed was he each time he played there.

Brown enjoyed his finest moments in cricket during the 1938 Ashes tour, when he made back-to-back centuries. This included his distinguished double on a peach of a wicket against a world-class attack including Ken Farnes, a young Douglas Wright, and the Yorkshire spin-master, Hedley Verity. His 133 at Trent Bridge in the opening Test had helped Australia force a draw, after England had started with 8/658 declared.

At Lord's just over a week later, he made 206, becoming the fifth Australian to carry his bat. It was, and remains, the highest unconquered score by an opener in Ashes history.

'I liked the Lord's wicket,' Brown said. 'Lord's has the atmosphere and the tradition and it tends to bring out whatever you have in you. The wicket was quicker than the average England wicket and played very truly. It was more like an Australian wicket. It suited me better than the slower wickets where you had to force the ball.'

BILL BROWN AT LORD'S

Year	Scores
1934	105 & 2
1938	206* & 10
1948	24 & 32
Total: 379 runs, 75.80 average	

* not out

AUSTRALIANS TO CARRY THEIR BAT IN ASHES BATTLES*

John Barrett	67, Lord's, 1890
Warren Bardsley	193, Lord's, 1926
Bill Woodfull	30, Brisbane (Exhibition Ground), 1928–29
Bill Woodfull	73, Adelaide, 1932–33
Bill Brown	206, Lord's, 1938
Bill Lawry	60, Sydney, 1970–71

* all not out

CASUALTY OF WAR

Ross Gregory's career was tragically short. He was the only Australian Test cricketer to lose his life during World War II, having enlisted with the RAAF and served in Europe and Burma. Originally from Gardenvale State School and Wesley College in Melbourne, he was slight of figure, just 171 cm (5'7") tall and, with his boyish looks, could travel unchallenged at a discount on the trains and trams far longer than many of his peers.

His highest first-class score, of 128, came against the MCC in 1936–37, when he partnered Ian Lee. In a stand of 262 over three unforgettable hours, Gregory's hook shots were superlative.

The more experienced Arthur Chipperfield was chosen over Gregory for the 1938 tour of England for his slip fielding abilities, and Gregory never received another opportunity. The plane on which he was navigating perished in a horrific storm near Ghafargan, Assam in India on 10 June 1942. All six aboard died. St Kilda Cricket Club named its No. 2 oval, adjoining the Junction Oval, in his honour.

CAUGHT IN THE CROSSFIRE

When Curtly Ambrose went around the wicket and bowled a stream of bouncers from about 21 yards against the Australian tail in Perth in 1996–97, his intentions were clear: to hurt anyone who got in his way, especially if his name was Shane Warne! Having been struck in the ribs by Glenn McGrath while batting on a dry and cracked pitch that resembled a crossword puzzle, big Curtly was keen to batter and bruise. With the Australian second innings disintegrating, he bowled one 12-ball over before tea and a 15-ball over immediately afterwards, overstepping by many feet.

'He was after Shane. I was caught in the crossfire . . . a victim of circumstance,' said fast bowler Andy Bichel. 'A big guy like that coming from around the wicket bowling off 19 or 20 yards [is scary]. You sometimes get that in the nets but not too often in the middle. There weren't too many balls on our half.'

Bichel and Warne showed pluck during their 55-run partnership, but the West Indies won easily, Ambrose taking seven wickets for the game and making the ball rear like a super-ball on the fastest wicket in the country.

A CENTURY WITHOUT HAVING TO RUN

Substituting for an injured Shane Warne at Hampshire in English county ranks in 2004, rising star Shane Watson made immediate headlines by scoring a century on debut – while batting the entire time with a runner! He'd torn a hamstring earlier in the match.

Others to score heavily, having been injured mid-innings, include England's Raman Subba Row, who scored 98 of his 137 against Australia at The Oval with the help of a runner; and Pakistan's Saeed Anwar, who made 127 of his stand-and-deliver 194 against India in Chennai with a runner.

CHAPPELLI'S BEST

Almost all the best bowlers Ian Chappell faced were fast men, like England's John Snow, South Africa's Mike Procter and Australia's own Graham 'Garth' McKenzie. Among the few spinners he rated was India's master of drift, Erapalli Prasanna, who dismissed him six times in two series.

'He was the best opposition spin bowler I ever played against,' Chappell said of Prasanna. 'He was very, very tough in '67–'68 [when India toured Australia]. But even a couple of years later, in India in 1969–70, when I'd established myself and had a great deal more confidence in my ability, I still found it bloody hard to get to him.

'I used to say to him, "You little bastard, Pras. You have a string on that ball. You let it go and as soon as you see me coming, you pull the bloody thing back!" I could never get to him. He was a very, very fine bowler.'

CHEEKY EDGAR

Edward, the Prince of Wales (later the Duke of Windsor) was a popular figure down-under, especially after his royal tour in 1920, when he thanked Australians for their participation in World War I.

When 'The Digger Prince' met Warwick Armstrong

and the 1921 touring Australians mid-match in Bristol, Edgar Mayne caused quite a stir by declining the Prince's offer of a drink – but, if the Prince could spare it, he'd love a cigar!

A CHRISTMAS TO REMEMBER

On the eve of Don Bradman's recall for the Melbourne Ashes Test of 1928–29, the young maestro made one and 71 not out for New South Wales against Victoria at the Melbourne Cricket Ground over Christmas week.

Not only did the Sheffield Shield game continue on Christmas Day, the sole instance of first-class cricket being played on the ground on December 25, it was notable for Alan Kippax's chanceless 260 not out and his record five-hour, 307-run partnership for the tenth wicket with tailender Hal Hooker. Together, in one of the most miraculous partnerships of all, they lifted NSW from a down-and-out 9/113, chasing 376, to first innings points.

The 31-year-old Kippax made 240, or almost 80 per cent of the wondrous stand – still the highest for the tenth wicket in first-class annals. Time and again he was able to 'farm' the strike, stealing singles from the last ball of an over, to the growing frustration of Jack Ryder and his Victorians. From lunch to tea on Christmas Day, Hooker advanced his score by just four – from 18 to 22.

As news of the great stand spread, the crowd grew substantially, to almost 15 000. Noted cricket writer Ray Robinson said many paid their admission using the threepences and sixpences they'd found in their Christmas puddings. Hooker was finally dismissed on Boxing Day morning for a career-best 62, having defied the odds for 304 minutes.

THE CHUCK AND ERNIE SHOW

Tired of others dropping dolly catches from his bowling during a harum-scarum tenth-wicket stand between Victorian tailenders 'Chuck' Fleetwood-Smith and Ernie McCormick (Melbourne, 1934), experienced Queenslander Ron Oxenham camped himself under a skyer from McCormick. 'Stay back – I'll catch it myself!' he ordered.

So high did the ball go that Oxenham had plenty of time. But just as he raised his hands to take the catch, he lost it. The ball bounced on his forehead and rolled away harmlessly. He was so furious that he gathered up the ball and tried for a run-out, only succeeding in giving away several overthrows.

'I got 77 [not out] that day, with five or six chances – by far my highest score,' said McCormick. 'No matter what Chuck or I did, we just couldn't get out.'

The pair added 98, with Fleetwood's 63 also a career-best effort.

CITY NO LURE FOR MURPH

Jamie Murphy is only half joking when he says his biggest moment in cricket was sitting next to a young Shane Warne in a premiership photo. Murphy won't hear a bad word against cricket's human headline.

'Some people knock Shane and they don't even know him,' Murphy said. 'I'd love to get those people to meet him so they could see for themselves. I saw him at Christmas time [2003] and he hadn't changed at all. He was still the same knockabout bloke and someone who is fiercely loyal to his family and friends.'

The pair had played together for St Kilda in the 1991–92 Melbourne district cricket final, when Murphy had made 41 and Warne, then 21, had taken two for 65 from 49 overs.

Murphy's most prolific year came in the big smoke,

when he made four centuries for the St Kilda seconds, only to flounder when promoted.

'Think I got a bit too nervous when I went up [to the firsts],' he said.

Having made the Victorian state squad and played in three first XI premierships at St Kilda, Murphy said 10 years in the city was enough, and returned to Moama with his young family. His most notable feat at country cricket level was to make 302 not out for Mathoura against the Rochester Tigers in 1996–97.

CLASSIC QUIPS (I)

Terry Jenner, fresh out of jail, was in Sydney to speak at an Ashes cricket breakfast. The speaker before him was Sir Oliver Popplewell, the president of the esteemed Marylebone Cricket Club and a judge of much standing. 'The last time I was invited to speak after a judge,' said Jenner, 'he gave me six-and-a-half years!'

CLASSIC QUIPS (II)

We were on tour at Amersham in '87 and I was congratulating one of their players, a petite young girl who, coming in at No. 4, had impressed us all.

'You know,' I said, 'you should stick with your cricket. You play very well indeed.'

Our 'keeper, Mark Foster, was within earshot and pulled me aside. 'Piessey, you bloody idiot,' he hissed at me. 'That's Jan Brittin. She opens the batting for England!'

CLOSE BUT NO CIGAR (I)

Bill Lawry sauntered down the wicket to Ian Redpath, who was playing his first Test (Melbourne, 1963–64). 'Watch [Joe] Partridge. He moves 'em,' said Lawry.

'Redders was on 93 at the time,' Lawry said later, 'and then played just about the best cover drive I'd ever seen to move to 97, only to get knocked over.'

In an otherwise fairytale start to his Test career against Trevor Goddard's South Africans, Redpath said he'd simply lost focus when it counted.

'The first 97 runs that day were very exciting,' he said. 'What should have been my hundredth turned out to be the end of my innings. I'd like to say it was a big inswinger but it was probably straight. I'd hit the previous ball for four and thought it was the same sort of delivery. Basically I was licking the chops and looking at the pickets just wide of the sightscreen [at Bay 13]. Had I been a little more patient, I might [have got there]. I was well in and seeing them okay.

'It wasn't so painful then to be dismissed three short of 100. At the time, I was rapt to get over 20 in my first Test match. I was probably more disappointed 30 years on.'

Then 22, Redpath wasn't told he was in the final XI until just 20 minutes before the game. 'Simmo [Australian captain Bob Simpson] came up and said, "You're in – and you're opening." I didn't have a lot of time to think about it.'

Despite his auspicious beginnings, Redpath was dropped from the next Test, a fit-again Normie O'Neill coming back into Australia's top three. However, he was to play 66 Tests and average almost 45 for Australia. On his retirement, in 1975–76, he was among Australia's top five all-time runmakers.

'Redders was the most underrated cricketer of my period,' said Simpson. 'He had something special. He was a very adaptable player, a real stylist early on, in the Paul Sheahan mould. But Paul was never able to adapt as well as Redders. When it got tough, Redders could adjust his shots. Most stylists can't do that.'

CLOSE BUT NO CIGAR (II)

According to Keith Stackpole jnr, his father, Keith snr, was a victim of the most powerful era in the first 100 years of Australian cricket. His chance of promotion into representative ranks was stymied by the depth of star players available immediately after World War II.

'He was a better cricketer than me,' said Stackpole jnr, who played 43 Tests. 'But he was in the Bradman era when there were so many good players around.'

In the late forties, Stacky snr made two centuries, both against South Australia in Adelaide on his way to more than 1000 first-class runs at an average of 35. He always claimed he was one of the lucky ones, as other fine players hadn't been able to break into Sheffield Shield ranks at all, while some – Cec Pepper, Bill Alley, Des Fothergill, Ken Grieves, Jack Manning, George Tribe, Jock Livingston and others – were lured to England to play. Fellow Melburnians like Percy Beames and Gordon Tamblyn were also good enough to play Test cricket at the time but, like Stackpole, lacked the opportunity.

A CLOSE CALL

Sportsmen live on a razor's edge. Even the elite ones. Mark Taylor had been bumbling along in the Australian side, out of form and seemingly friendless, when he came to the momentous decision to drop himself.

Having failed in the first innings of an otherwise inconsequential county game at Derby in 1997, he went for a wide half-volley early in the second innings, hardly moving his feet, and the resultant nick lobbed at highly catchable pace towards Derbyshire's captain, Australian Dean Jones, at slip. Taylor had time to watch it arc into Jones's hands and was preparing to walk off when, inexplicably, the chance was grassed.

Taylor felt little satisfaction at his reprieve and, at the end-of-over, told his partner, Justin Langer, 'Well, that's about it. I'm just about ready to give up.' The nightmares of the extended Australian summer, coupled with an even poorer run in the opening weeks in England and the constant media quizzing as to his future, had so sapped Taylor's morale that he was ready to stand down, then and there.

Langer, a junior member of the team, blinked and said, 'That's rubbish, absolute rubbish. Just watch the ball. You'll be right.'

From a shaky nine not out at tea, Taylor finished at 59 not out at stumps, only his second half-century in eight months since returning from back surgery. He'd played a couple of meaty drives and even a couple of leg-side flicks, every opener's bread and butter. By stumps, he was actually enjoying himself again.

A week later, having deflected more broadsides and condemnation after his and Australia's slow start in the first Test, he made a back-to-the-wall century in the second innings at Edgbaston and, by the fifth Test at Trent Bridge, the Australians had not only reclaimed the Ashes, Taylor had resurrected his career.

'It all hinged on that catch that day at Derby,' Taylor said. 'If Deano hadn't dropped me at slip, maybe I would have been finished as an international cricketer. That's how close it was.'

COKES ALL ROUND

It was a case of Cokes all round after the 300-plus target set by Central Park/St Brendan's was reached, in the summer of 2003. Cokes? Well, the winners were from Dhurringile Prison in Murchison, country Victoria. Drinking anything stronger was taboo.

COMPARING THE CHAPPELLS

Ian Redpath: *Greg was superior [to Ian] on good wickets. If he got 20, you knew he'd get 70 or 80. He was that good. Ian Chappell was a very adaptable player at No. 3. He could put the shutters up and fight hard if there was an early wicket, or he could come in and accelerate. He was also an excellent all-round cricketer.*

COOLING HIS HEELS

After a lifetime in the game, veteran umpire David Shepherd reckons he has just about seen it all. But even he was amazed when his partner, the zany New Zealander Billy Bowden, took off his boots and calmly put them in the refrigerator during the luncheon breaks of the 2003 Christmas Test in Melbourne.

It's one of Bowden's many idiosyncrasies – along with his crooked finger when giving batsmen out, and his unique method of signalling sixes. Bowden says cricketers – and umpires – are in the entertainment industry. Why not smile and show everyone he's enjoying himself, too?

And the shoes-in-the-fridge thing? 'It's just something I do,' he says.

CORNERING THE HEADLINES

Arthur Morris's big century at The Oval in 1948 was an unforgettable finale to Australia's unbeaten 1948 tour of England. But it was Don Bradman's second-ball duck in his last Test innings that truly cornered the headlines. Years later, Morris remembered the moment.

'I was at a business conference and I don't think these people knew much about cricket. Someone said how Don Bradman got a duck in his last innings and I said I knew 'cos I was there.'

'What were you doing over there? Business? Holidays?' asked one delegate.

'Actually, I was up the other end,' Morris replied.

'Did you get any runs?'

'Yes . . . actually, I did. 196!'

CRAWLING AT KARACHI

Keith Miller playing and missing five times in a row? Surely not! But it happened during 'the Karachi Crawl' in 1956, when a record-low 95 runs were made on the opening day's play between Australia and Pakistan.

Coming off an arduous tour of England, the Australians played an inaugural Test against the Pakistanis and three against the Indians as their tour extended into a ninth month. Batting first on a coir matting wicket, the Australians took more than 50 overs to make just 80, with Fazel Mahmood taking six for 34 with fast leg-cutters, and Khan Mohammad four for 43 with off-cutters. So commanding were these two that they bowled unchanged throughout the Australian innings.

In his last Test match, Miller top-scored with 21, but played at Fazel and missed five times in a row, underlining the menace of batting in such challenging conditions. In an interview with cricket writer Mark Browning, Ian Craig said he was one of several of the Australians who had never seen a matting wicket, let alone played on one.

'We'd played for months on damp turf pitches in England, having to contend with champion spinners like Jim Laker and Tony Lock,' he said. 'Then we arrived in Pakistan and immediately had to adopt a totally different batting technique. The weather, too, was hotter and more physically demanding. Drink breaks would be taken every 40 minutes and, each time, they would bring out salt tablets for us.

'The bowling of Fazel and Khan, though, was the main factor. They were amazing and a total revelation. They seamed the ball all over the place and at pace, Fazel being like a fast leg-spinner and Khan a fast off-spinner. There was only one boundary scored during the entire Australian innings, with the wicket exceptionally slow, the ground large and the outfield surprisingly lush.'

So tough was it defending, let alone looking to score, that Craig took almost 50 minutes over a duck and said he was mentally exhausted at the end of the innings.

To top it all off, on the last day of the Test, Ron Archer went over on his knee when one of his spikes caught in the matting. The injury effectively ended his career – and his national captaincy aspirations.

CRICKET LISTS

TEN NICKNAMES

- Steve Bernard, 'Brute' (after the wrestler)
- Don Blackie, 'Rock' (he called everyone 'Rock')
- Michael Clarke, 'Pup' (the youngest in the team)
- Grahame Corling, 'I'llbe' (from the song 'I'll Be Calling You')
- John Gleeson, 'Cho' (cricket hours only)
- Bert Ironmonger, 'Dainty' (he wasn't)
- Bill Lawry, 'Phant' or 'Phanto' (he packed *Phantom* comics into his bags on his first trip away)
- Dennis Lillee, 'Fot' (former captain, Tony Lock, once accused him of bowling like 'a flippin' old tart')
- Bob Massie, 'Ferg' (after the Massey-Ferguson tractor)
- Paul Sheahan, 'Timbers' (he attended Geelong Grammar School's elite Timbertop campus)
- Mark Waugh, 'June' or 'Junior' (he was born just minutes after his twin brother, Stephen)

Ten of Australian Cricket's Most Controversial Axings

- Don Bradman, 1928
- Keith Miller, 1949
- Sid Barnes, 1951
- Graham McKenzie, 1967
- Bill Lawry, 1971
- Dirk Wellham, 1981
- Geoff Marsh, 1992
- Shane Warne, 1999
- Ian Healy, 1999
- Martin Love, 2003

Ten of the Best Never to Play Test Cricket

- Bill Alley (NSW)
- Percy Beames (Vic.)
- Darren Berry (SA & Vic.)
- Sid Carroll (NSW)
- Jamie Cox (Tas.)
- 'Sunny' Jim Mackay (NSW)
- Cec Pepper (NSW)
- Jamie Siddons* (Vic. & SA)
- Frank Tarrant (Vic.)
- Sam Trimble (Qld)

* played a one-day international

Ten of the Best to Miss Ashes Tours in Controversial Circumstances

- Jack Harry, 1890 & 1896
- Albert Trott, 1896
- Alan Kippax, 1926
- Jack Ryder, 1930
- Ken Meuleman, 1948
- Geff Noblet, 1953
- Barry Shepherd, 1964

- Terry Jenner, 1972
- Graham McKenzie, 1972
- Michael Whitney, 1989

TEN AUSTRALIAN TOURISTS
WHO NEVER PLAYED A TEST

- Charlie Walker, England, 1938
- E. S. 'Ted' White, England, 1938
- Alan Walker (NSW), South Africa, 1949–50
- Jack Potter (Vic.), England, 1964
- Gordon Becker (WA), South Africa, 1966–67
- Jim Hubble (WA), South Africa, 1966–67
- Jock Irvine (WA), India & South Africa, 1969–70
- Graeme Porter (WA), India, 1979–80
- Jamie Siddons (Vic.), Pakistan, 1988–89
- Wayne Holdsworth (NSW), England, 1993

TEN HIGHEST BATTING AVERAGES IN ENGLAND

- Steve Waugh, 167.31, 1993
- Don Bradman, 115.66, 1938
- Damien Martyn, 104.66, 2001
- Bill Johnston, 102.00, 1953
- Don Bradman, 98.66, 1930
- Don Bradman, 89.92, 1948
- Dean Jones, 88.82, 1989
- Don Bradman, 84.16, 1934
- Bill Ponsford, 77.56, 1934
- David Boon, 75.63, 1993

Note: The highest early average in England was Victor Trumper's 48.49 in 1902, an extraordinarily high average on uncovered wickets.

CROWD-PLEASER

Until Kerry Packer came along with $25 000 for three months of rebel cricket down-under in 1977, sightings of Barry Richards in Australia were all too rare. He was 30-plus but still an all-star, as he proved with an imperious double-century against the World Series Australians at Gloucester Park and an 80 average in the Supertests.

In the early seventies, Richards was one of the few genuine challengers to Greg Chappell as the premier batsman in the world. He had been denied an Australian tour with Ali Bacher's Springboks in 1971–72, after apartheid became a world issue and South Africa was banned from international cricket. Excluding some Perth grade appearances, the first year of World Series was the South African master's only visit to Australia, other than his six-month Sheffield Shield stint in Adelaide in 1970–71.

'At the time, we'd just had a tour cancelled and I wondered would I ever get to Australia if I didn't go now?' he said. 'It was an opportunity. I was single at the time. I thought, why not?'

What a summer it proved for Richards: more than 1500 first-class runs and another 500 at grade level – and all at $1 a run, courtesy of his Coca-Cola sponsorship.

'Ian Chappell and the other South Australian guys were happy that I was scoring runs and that we were winning games,' Richards said. 'They realised I was a professional cricketer and that's how I earned my livelihood. In those days, we were getting $40 per game, too, which I thought an absolute bonus. When I played with Natal [in South Africa], we got nothing.'

The most memorable week in his phenomenal summer of tall scores came in Perth in mid-November 1970, when he scored 325 runs on the opening day on his way to 356, the first-ever triple-century at the West Australian Cricket Association (WACA) Ground. The mega-scoring Bill Ponsford had also scored 300 runs in a day of Sheffield Shield, 45 years previously, but he had more of the strike than Richards, given that Victoria faced almost 25 per cent more overs in a day's play.

So dominant was South Australia's star import that captain Ian Chappell's 129 was totally overshadowed. Dennis Lillee rated Richards' display with Sir Garfield Sobers' 254 a year later as the finest of his time. Not only did Richards score at an express run-a-ball pace, he batted with the aplomb of a Mark Waugh. His stroke-play was truly exquisite against a crack attack of Lillee, Graham McKenzie, Tony Mann, Tony Lock, John Inverarity and Ian Brayshaw.

Richards volleyed the last ball of the afternoon straight back over Lillee's head into the sightscreen – a glorious shot only a champion in supreme form would consider, let alone execute, against a bowler of Lillee's pace and temper. Richards scored 81 in the first session, 137 in the second and 109 in the third. Had a full two hours been allocated in the opening sessions in Shield cricket in those days, Richards may well have made centuries in all three sessions.

'It wasn't the best I'd ever played, but it was for the length of time I batted,' Richards said. 'Big scores were never my go. The object of the game, to me, was to score as quickly as I could and the risks are much higher when you do that. I'd like to think that people remember me not just as a good player, but as someone they'd like to go and see.'

d
||||||||||||

DANCIN' MAN

No one was as nimble or took on the spinners as success-fully as Neil Harvey, the world's finest batsman for most of the fifties. Harvey thanks Joe Plant, his former coach at Fitzroy Cricket Club, for advancing his game to fresh levels while he was a teenager.

'Joe had played for Victoria in the thirties as an off-spin bowler and, after he left Fitzroy, he also coached at South Melbourne,' Harvey said. 'He was instrumental in get-ting me to use my feet a lot better than I would have done otherwise. He gave me a lot of practice on Tuesdays and Thursdays, for hours and hours. He'd use a hanky or a coin, whatever was available at the time, as a target.'

'C'mon son,' Joe would say to Harvey. 'Let's see how quick you can get down to that [target].'

Harvey said he was never stumped in a Test, and only occasionally at minor level, when he had virtually thrown his innings away. Again and again, he would venture down the wicket to attack the bowling, prompting the Englishman Tom Goddard to ask, 'Where do you bowl to this chap?'

SEE: 'WHO LEADS YOU OUT TO BAT?', PAGE 226

DEVOTION AND DEDICATION

No one was more passionate about cricket, or had a big-ger mailbag, than Sir Donald Bradman. Well into his eighties, he was still answering up to 200 letters a week. According to Bobby Simpson, who was given two captaincy stints during his celebrated career, Bradman was as big a champion off the field as he was on it.

'He attended hundreds of meetings, was a selector and was chairman of the [Australian Cricket] Board for so long,' Simpson said. 'He'd come into the dressing room when Richie [Benaud] was captain or when I was captain and if you wanted to have a talk – fine. If not, he'd wander off and have his lunch. He was always particularly helpful. When you spoke, he'd always give you a detailed explanation and, if you wrote to him, you'd get a long letter giving all the points. How many people in life have answered every letter they've ever got? And he got tens of thousands more than anyone else. It says a lot about a man who cared so much for the game and the people who followed it.'

DIVINE INTERVENTION

But for the intervention of Don Bradman, lean and long Bill Johnston may have concentrated purely on his left-arm slows and never truly fulfilled his promise. Promoted into senior club ranks in Melbourne as a slow bowler, Johnston was one of the leading wicket-takers at district level before being asked to bowl fast in the absence of anyone else.

Bradman was managing South Australia's XI during an interstate match at St Kilda in 1945–46 and was particularly impressed by Johnston's opening burst, which included wickets in his first two overs.

'I bowled spinners in that game as well,' said Johnston, 'and Don had a word to me at lunch on the final day. "I've watched you bowl, Bill," he said, "but I don't know if you spin the ball enough on first-class wickets. If you are interested in improving your game, you'd be better off organising your fast bowling and concentrating on that. There are not too many fast bowlers around at the moment, but there are quite a few spinners."

'Shortly afterwards, I was down at the Old Scotch Ground one night, practising with the Colts, when Jack Ryder [ex-Australian Test captain] asked me to bowl fast at him.

'I had no great control, but I bowled faster and at one stage I thought I almost knocked his head off. He was in his mid-fifties then. Thankfully, he got out of the road. It must have impressed him, as he reckoned I should have been able to bowl eight balls an over fast, rather than just one or two. I told him it was too much like hard work and I didn't want to do it. But he persisted.'

Ironically, Johnston had been selected to make his first-class debut four years earlier, but the bombing of Pearl Harbor meant that all major cricket had to be abandoned immediately.

'DO YOU KNOW WHAT YOU'VE JUST DONE, GRUM?'

From midway through his first season, Don Bradman was the ultimate drawcard in every match he played. In the era of testimonial matches between the wars, it was always advantageous to have the Don bat after lunch, when the crowd was at its biggest.

When Victor Richardson and his great South Australian colleague Clarrie Grimmett were granted a testimonial in 1937–38, there was great anticipation as Bradman skipped down the members' steps and on to Adelaide Oval. It was just after midday on the last Friday in November.

However, having batted for just half an hour, Bradman was out, deceived by 45-year-old Grimmett. Richardson marched up to Grimmett with tears in his eyes.

'Do you know what you've just done, Grum?' said Richardson.

'Yes, I've just bowled Don with my leg-break!'

'You've just cost us thousands of pounds,' said Richardson.

Hundreds of workers would no longer bother spending their afternoon at the cricket, knowing that the Don was already out. However, Richardson and Grimmett still grossed £1028 each, with more than 15 000 attending the opening two days.

SEE: EVERYONE WANTED DON, PAGE 64

THE DON ON STRIKE

Don Bradman on strike? It sounds inconceivable but Australia's sporting icon was not making an idle threat. As a result, he almost missed the most infamous Ashes series of all, the 1932–33 Bodyline summer.

It was the height of the Depression and Bradman was grateful to accept a substantial three-tiered contract to write and commentate on the game. However, the austere Australian Cricket Board of Control disapproved and, having missed the first Test of the summer through illness, Bradman was ready to stand out of the game altogether before Frank Packer (Kerry's father) released him from the agreement.

'We want you to play,' Packer said.

In his first game back, in Melbourne, Bradman made a century and Australia won their only match of a very acrimonious summer.

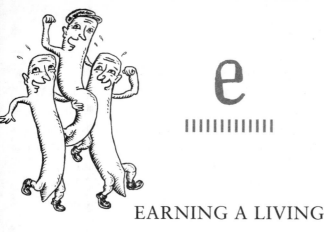

e
||||||||||||

EARNING A LIVING

Studies were rarely more than a diversion for the Waugh twins, Stephen and Mark. Their compelling interest in sport overshadowed all else and they excelled in virtually everything they did, from cricket and soccer through to tennis. They were naturals.

Named the New South Wales Young Sportsman of the Year in 1984, Steve, then 19, wanted to see how far he could progress – particularly with cricket, his number one sport. The opportunity of seeing the world and being paid for the privilege had particular appeal. Soccer had also been an option, and he was regarded as a genuine prospect. But when Sydney Croatia told him he could play in the first-grade team only if he specialised, he stopped altogether.

A half-day of lectures at college and some labouring with a road crew convinced Steve that he must earn a living *his* way. Mark soon followed and, between them, they were to represent Australia more than 800 times.

EAST–WEST WICKETS

The first wicket table at the famed Melbourne Cricket Ground was pitched in an east–west direction, only to be changed in 1881 after 'Felix' (Tom Horan) commented in the *Australasian* that a growing number of players were complaining about how difficult it was batting from the eastern end – especially late in the day, when the sun was setting.

But instead of being positioned exactly north–south, like the wicket tables at other major mainland venues, the MCG wickets were positioned just west of north and east of south. Ex-Test captain and opening batsman Bobby Simpson, a regular visitor to Melbourne, always got the feeling that the wickets faced the wrong direction.

'I've got a good sense of direction, usually,' he said, 'but I always thought that something wasn't quite right here.'

'ELEVEN TO EIGHT AGAINST!'

Ex-Victorian swing specialist and, later, Australian team manager, John Edwards was a legendary leader at St Kilda Cricket Club. He was known to pen his batting line-up in order of arrival and, when a particularly tough-to-catch skyer went up, would often call, 'Eleven to eight against!'

Players who dared apply for a clearance would be told, at the top of Edwards' voice and invariably in front of others, that if they didn't want to play at the club, 'then we don't want you, anyway!'

Jovial and universally liked, Edwards loved to hold court over a bottle or two of red at Victorian state matches, regaling all with tall stories and true.

'He was a beauty,' said ex-Testman Rodney Hogg. 'Even into his fifties, he'd bowl these big inswingers at practice.

'Dennis Lillee was known as "Fot" and John turned that into "Lord Fotbury". He was simply a brilliant bloke.'

Edwards filled in for St Kilda's fourth XI one day, playing alongside his son, Peter. For old time's sake, he opened the bowling.

'He took the first seven or eight wickets and had to take himself off to give someone else a bowl,' said Peter.

AN ENDURING PARTNERSHIP

Unlike her husband and long-time Australian Prime Minister Robert Menzies, Dame Pattie Menzies had little understanding of cricket. Asked one day if she had actually been to a match, she said she had – in Melbourne in 1924–25, when Jack Hobbs and Herbert Sutcliffe batted through an entire day's play.

'I got bored and went home in the afternoon,' she said. 'We were in England in 1926 and Bob suggested I should see at least one game in England, so down to The Oval I went, Australia playing England, and there they were again, Hobbs and Sutcliffe. They were still batting!'

EVEN JOEL LAUGHED

In the early 1980s, fast bowlers at the MCG could rarely make the ball bounce stump-high, so lifeless was the wicket, especially from mid-match onwards. Lenny Pascoe bowled more short balls than most and, seeing the 203-centimetre (6'9") Joel Garner take block in a one-dayer, decided to give him one.

'I came in and let this thing go with all the energy I could. It was the slowest, balloonist bouncer you've ever seen. But it did manage to go over the top of Joel's head and everyone started laughing, even Joel, especially as it very nearly bowled him. Up until then, none of us had been able to get it much more than shin-high.

'Rod Marsh came down at the end of the over, a huge grin on his face and said, "You had to try, didn't you? You had to try!"'

SEE: QUICK FROM NINETEEN YARDS, PAGE 166

EVERYONE WANTED DON

Emerging opening batsman Bill Brown was in his 70s when Don Bradman joined him at the wicket. New South Wales was playing Victoria in Sydney and, as always, the contest was keen. The second new ball was due within the hour.

'Bill,' Bradman said to Brown, 'we must get your hundred before the next new ball.' And Bradman proceeded to take singles.

Enjoying the extra strike, Brown duly made his hundred, with Bradman on just 15 or 16.

'Guess what happened next!' said Brown, years later. 'By the time I was into my 120s, Don had passed me. And all in less than an hour's play. He really went for it that day.'

As NSW's opener, Brown says his job was to take the shine off the new ball for those who followed. But if he happened to bat too long, the crowd would become restless.

'Once they lit a fire on The Hill, and it spread to the Sheridan Stand,' said Brown. 'And if you happened to get hit on the pads, the whole crowd would go up with the bowler for the lbw! You'd get this huge ovation as you were going off. Everyone wanted Don.'

EXPRESS EDDIE

'Luckiest duck I ever made,' said a young Don Bradman, when asked about falling to the withering pace of Queenslander Eddie Gilbert in 1931–32. Bradman lasted just four balls before edging the fifth through to the wicketkeeper in a Sheffield Shield match in Brisbane.

Gilbert ambled in from just five or six paces and preferred to bowl in bare feet. His dislike of city living was immense and, in between Queensland fixtures, he often preferred to play his Saturday cricket back at Barambah.

FAMILY FIRST

Four of Greg Chappell's 24 Test centuries came in Melbourne, including one of the most memorable, against Mike Brearley's Englishmen in 1979–80. On the final afternoon, Australia needed just 103 and Chappell, who had promoted himself to No. 4, had one eye on the scoreboard and another on the clock as he sailed into the bowling.

'It was an important stage of the game and Ian [Chappell] and I were batting together,' said Greg. 'I had a young family and had been away from home for a few weeks. There was an opportunity to catch a flight late in the afternoon or I'd have to wait until the next morning.

'I said to Ian I was going to try and start to pick up the tempo a little bit and see if we could finish the game that afternoon. I felt Derek Underwood was the bowler I could get to most, under those conditions. I decided to get aggressive and we scored the runs fairly quickly. We managed to get the game over and done with that afternoon, in time for me to catch the flight.'

Chappell's 40 came from just 43 balls, with the final 61 winning runs coming in well under an hour. His match double – of 114 and 40 not out – lifted his summer aggregate to almost 600 runs, maintaining his position (alongside the West Indian Viv Richards) as the outstanding batsman in the world.

SEE: GREG CHAPPELL'S FIRST TEST, PAGE 89

A FAMOUS LOSS

Allan Border was big on hunches. The thousands gathering at the MCG on the final morning of the 1982–83 Christmas Test, despite Australia's plight, raised even his expectations. Maybe Australia *could* win from nowhere.

At 9/218, chasing 292, an Australian win had seemed out of the question late on Day Four, as No. 11 batsman Jeff Thomson ambled to the crease. Teammates Rod Marsh and David Hookes were so sure of an English win that they left their seats and showered and dressed, ready for a quick exit. With 74 runs still needed, Border rated Australia's winning chances as 1000 to one. But, somehow, he and 'Thommo' made it to stumps, halving the target to 37.

The Australians dispensed with their normal warm-up on the final morning, Thomson and Border the only two bothering to have a net. They were greeted by roars of appreciation as they emerged down the race. Thommo turned to his mate and said, 'If it's good enough for all these people to come along, we should f—ing well go for it, mate.'

Clearly motivated to support his specialist batting partner – then in a trough of low scores – Thommo played successive maidens from the fourth-day destroyer Norman Cowans. Applause echoed around the ground for defensive pushes, and rose to a crescendo for one theatrical leave. Just five runs were scored in the dramatic first half-hour.

More and more fans raced to vantage spots, making the most of the free admission. But it wasn't until England's captain, Bob Willis, introduced the second new ball that the run-rate increased, with Thomson and Border playing more freely and running for some sharp singles. The English panicked in the field. Allan Lamb collided mid-pitch with substitute fieldsman Ian Gould as the target fell below 20.

By midday, the crowd was 18000 and there were traffic jams all round the precinct. Border and Thomson had revived memories of the remarkable tenth wicket stand between Bill Johnston and Doug Ring against the West Indies, also in Melbourne, 30 years earlier.

Willis opted to set deep fields for Border, conceding him singles, before crowding Thomson with close-in fieldsmen. When Border greeted Ian Botham's arrival with a drive for three to yet again corner the strike, just six were needed. Most of the fans were now standing and roaring their approval. Two more to Border from Willis reduced the target to four, leaving Thomson on strike to Botham.

Seeing the first ball short and wide, Thomson went for a square cut, but could only edge the ball. Standing at the non-striker's end, Border initially thought the ball was flying over the top of the slips, before it looped, was juggled by Chris Tavaré, and ultimately caught on the rebound by an ecstatic Geoff Miller. England had won by three runs in an extraordinary finish – the closest Melbourne Test on record.

Both Border, who'd made a career-saving 62 not out, and Thomson, 21, were heroes in defeat. For the first time in any Test match, the four innings totals were within a range of 10 runs: England 284 and 294; Australia 287 and 288.

Asked about Botham's final, match-winning wicket, Willis said, 'Golden bullocks got lucky . . . again!'

'FANCY DOING THAT'

It only ever happened once, but Leo O'Brien used to dine out on the time he batted at No. 3 ahead of Don Bradman (Melbourne, 1932–33).

'It was my first Test and Woody [Bill Woodfull] came in and said he'd won the toss and we were batting. I had my fielding creams on and, having looked at the order, went and changed into my batting trousers. I was in at three, behind Woody and Jack Fingleton,' remembers O'Brien.

'My kit was alongside Braddles, and Don was also changing. I put my right pad on first, then my left, and noticed he was also padding up. Looking across at me, he said, "You don't seem to have a lot of confidence in me, Leo!"

'He obviously thought he was in at the fall of the [first] wicket. I told him I'd had a look at the batting order and was down for three. Obviously I was there for a quick fall of wicket. Don just took his pads off and walked away without saying a word.

'That was the game he made the first-ball duck, dragging one on [from Bill Bowes]. I was still taking my gear off when he came back in. "Fancy doing that," was all he said.'

A FARTING GOOD PARTNERSHIP

In more than 10 years with the ABC, Lindsay Hassett reckons it was his pièce de résistance: the time he referred, on radio, to a fine, fighting partnership between Queenslanders Ken Mackay and Peter Burge as 'a fine, farting partnership'.

SEE: LOVABLE LINDSAY, PAGE 123

FAST AND FIERY . . . AT ELEVEN!

Brad Williams's first cricket coach, with the Baxter Under 12s on Melbourne's Mornington Peninsula, was Marilyn Harvey, mother of St Kilda AFL (Australian Football League) legend Robert Harvey.

'Brad was a fiery little character, even then,' Marilyn

said. 'He had the longest run-up and was always going to try and bowl fast. If anything, though, at that stage he stood out more as a batsman than as a bowler.'

When the Williams family moved to Mt Eliza, Brad's father, Clive, made sure that the backyard was long enough for a fair dinkum pitch, including a run-up.

'Clive was such a great support for Brad and all the kids,' said Mrs Harvey. 'He'd drive them everywhere and give them encouragement awards. He just loved it.'

During his first state game, as a teenager, Williams struck Allan Border on the elbow and forced him to retire hurt for the only time in his career. Williams promised to be the next big thing in Australian cricket.

But injuries interfered and, as he struggled for consistent recognition, it was Clive who encouraged him to expand his horizons and think about shifting interstate if it meant progressing his career. Clive died the year Williams moved to Perth. In 2003–04, when he made his Test debut in Sydney, Williams kissed the ball and looked skyward, honouring his dad.

A FAVOURITE FROM CHAPPELLI

It was Ian Chappell's first match as South Australia's captain and, at the toss with his West Australian counterpart, ex-English Testman Tony Lock, the coin landed on its side and rolled over to the other side of the pitch.

Walking to it first, Chappell said, 'It's heads, Tony. Do you wanna see it?'

'No, laard,' said Lock. 'But if you'd been Bill Lawry I would 'ave!'

FAVOURITES FROM FAVELLI (I)

Having hooked New Zealander Bob Blair into a grandstand at Christchurch (1957), buccaneering Les Favell sauntered down the other end and said, 'I hope they don't take you off!'

At Wellington, cricket writer Ray Robinson reported that Favell, piqued when his appeal against the light was rejected, struck four thunderous fours in the following over, all the time complaining about how dark it was. Umpire Jack Cowie asked him whether he could really see the ball or whether he was batting from memory!

FAVOURITES FROM FAVELLI (II)

Eric Freeman loved to get on with it and, with one century in less than 90 minutes for the Australians at Northampton in 1968, and another from just 23 balls in an up-country match at Mt Gambier, his hitting could be spectacular. But one mid-sixties day, against the Victorians at the Adelaide Oval, he miscalculated and sent a steepling catch to the clouds and back. Even before the catch was accepted, he began to march off the ground – the *wrong* way.

'Les [then South Australian captain] had told me just before I went out, "If you get out to a big hit, Fritz, don't bother coming back."'

'So I didn't. I walked off through the Victor Richardson Gates and snuck around the back of the ground and up the back stairs . . . where Les was waiting for me with his arms folded!'

FAVOURITES FROM FAVELLI (III)

South Australia had hardly won all year and, having fielded into a sixth session in 32°C heat in Brisbane, was odds-on to be rolled again.

'It's still a fantastic batting wicket,' said Favell, attempting to lift morale. 'We can get these runs. It's just a matter of getting our heads down and working hard.'

John Lill was in at No. 3 and had only just finished buckling on his pads when there was a shout. Favell had succumbed in the second over. The score? 1/23.

'He'd gone *bang, bang, bang*, and walked past me muttering that he'd just missed the opportunity for another four!' said Lill. 'He loved getting on with it.'

Another time, according to Lill, South Australia was playing NSW and Les had reached 87 – the devil's number for cricketers. Normie O'Neill had sauntered past Favell and said, 'Guess what you're on, Les?'

'Yeah, 87,' said Favell, 'and I'll be 91 after this next ball!'

FIFTEEN MINUTES OF FAME (I)

Rodney Hogg claims to be the only ex-milkman ever to toss the coin for Australia.

'It was a one-dayer against India in the World Championship of Cricket [in 1985],' Hogg said. 'I'd been vice-captain to AB [Allan Border] for a couple of the Tests, and he was a little unwell this afternoon and asked me to go out.

'I didn't do too well – I lost it. We got sent in and were rock-and-rolled for 160-odd, and were beaten by eight wickets. AB never asked me again, but at least I got my name in *Wisden* as having tossed the coin!'

SEE: MADDER THAN MOST, PAGE 125

FIFTEEN MINUTES OF FAME (II)

Shaun Graf, twelfth man in two Tests in 1980–81, says he was grateful for the opportunity just to field during his time with Australia's elite XI.

'Some twelfthies never even get on. But I did, in Sydney, when Greg Chappell was off-colour. Kapil Dev hit one down my throat at long-on in front of the Bradman Stand. It went way up and I was pretty happy to hang on to it.'

Graf says he soon learnt, as twelfth man, how to mix Dennis Lillee's Sustagen drinks. 'Nine teaspoons [of powder] weren't enough. You had to have a tenth in there . . . otherwise you'd hear about it!' he said.

SEE: REBUKED BY THE DON, PAGE 171

FIFTEEN MINUTES OF FAME (III)

Colin Miller couldn't believe it. Here he was in faraway Antigua, and four Australian supporters, sporting 'Funky Miller Fan Club' T-shirts, were waving and cheering outside the ground at St John's. Not only did Miller ask the bus driver to stop, he hopped out, shared a beer, and had his picture taken with his fans while his Australian teammates – from the Waughs to Warnie – enjoyed the moment.

Colin Miller's cricketing renaissance was truly extraordinary – especially as he never seriously pursued slow bowling until he was 32. A genuine two-in-one bowler in the mould of Garry Sobers or Bill Johnston, Miller was to win Australia's Test Player of the Year award in 2001, at the ripe old age of 37. While he fell short of becoming Australia's first 40-year-old Test cricketer since Bobby Simpson, the fun-loving cricketing journeyman got to play at most of the major venues, including the Christmas Test in his home town of Melbourne. He maintained a keen involvement, too, as an occasional coach, tour host and selector on the national umpiring panel.

SEE: 'WHO DAT NEW BOWLER, MAAN?', PAGE 225

THE FINEST – BEFORE WARNE

Bill 'Tiger' O'Reilly loved Clarrie Grimmett. He nick-named him 'Grum' and taught him to drink. In one series, against the South Africans in 1935–36, Tiger took 27 wickets and Grum (aged 43 at the time!) took 44. Even Shane Warne's meteoric rise in 1991 failed to mask the Tiger's long-held view that Grimmett was the finest leg-spinner earthlings had seen.

The first to take 200 Test wickets, Grimmett boasted a career strike rate of 67 balls per wicket, teasing and tempting the batsmen, and being an ideal foil for O'Reilly's intimidating, bouncy breaks.

'Clarrie could size up a batsman in a few deliveries,' said O'Reilly. 'He had this little, skippy run and would concentrate on bowling straight at the stumps and land-ing the ball in the chosen awkward spot which demanded expert use of the feet.'

Grimmett was so accurate that almost one in two of his wickets were bowled or lbw. He was forever scheming and planning, his skidding top-spinner becom-ing his signature ball, just like Shane Warne's slider.

Before he met O'Reilly, Grimmett had been a teetotaller. 'I soon helped change all that!' said the Tiger.

CLARRIE GRIMMETT'S WICKETS

Bowled	25.9%
Caught	33.8%
Caught & bowled	5.1%
Caught behind	4.2%
LBW	17.6%
Stumped	13%
Hit wicket	0.5%

CLARRIE GRIMMETT: HOME AND AWAY

	Mts	Wkts	Ave	Best	5WI	10WM
Home	19	105	24.59	7/83	9	3
Away	18	111	23.86	7/40	12	4
Total	37	216	24.21	7/40	21	7

WI = wickets in an innings; WM = wickets in a match

THE FIRST 'BALL OF THE CENTURY'

Before Shane Warne's 'Ball of the Century', which skittled Mike Gatting at Old Trafford in 1993, the most celebrated single delivery in Ashes annals was delivered by another 'wristie', 'Chuck' Fleetwood-Smith (Adelaide, 1936–37). Set 391 runs to re-win the Ashes, England was 3/148 at close of play, with master batsman Wally Hammond 39 not out. As the Australians walked out to field on the sixth day, Don Bradman gave Fleetwood-Smith the ball.

Fleetwood responded with a big-spinning Chinaman that curved and spun back sharply, bowling Hammond without any addition to his overnight score. England was to make just 243, as Australia squared the series in Adelaide and went on to win the decider in Melbourne. With 10 wickets for the game, Fleetwood had been the matchwinner.

'[Hammond's wicket] probably turned the whole of that Test match in our favour,' said Bradman. 'Normally, it was difficult to get him [Fleetwood] to knuckle down and concentrate . . . he just wasn't that kind of fellow . . . [But] he took his cricket seriously that morning.'

Teammate Ernie McCormick said Bradman had addressed the players the previous night, saying, 'We've got to get this fella out early tomorrow because he can make a million. He's in one of his moods.' Fleetwood's response was typically breezy. 'She'll be right, Charlie!'

Ironically, it had been Hammond who, four years

earlier, had been most responsible for delaying Fleet-wood's entry into Test ranks, after he made a rapid-fire 203 against Victoria.

In his book *Cricket My World*, Hammond writes, 'When we were touring Australia in 1932, [Douglas] Jardine came to me and said, "The Victorians are trying out young Fleetwood-Smith. I don't want him chosen for the Tests – he could upset us badly – you've got to 'murder' him."'

Hammond said he took considerable risks to stall Fleetwood's entry into big cricket. Fleetwood's figures blew out to two for 124 from just 25 overs.

'England's batsmen knew he was ready in 1932,' said Hammond. 'But these things have to be done when orders are received and are done by all countries, though individuals may suffer.'

FISH 'N' CHIPS, STEAK AND A FEW SOFTIES

The best part of his Sheffield Shield debut (February, 1993), according to prolific Victorian Matthew Elliott, was that he could have fish 'n' chips or steak for lunch, and free softies from the players' fridge whenever he wanted.

'This is pretty good, I thought. It was my first-ever game at the MCG and it was really something just to be in the same rooms as people like O'Donnell, Reiffel, Dodemaide, Lehmann, Deano and Chuck Berry,' said Elliott. 'It was a bit intimidating at the same time . . . Many had played Test cricket and were all big names. I snuck into the rooms and headed down the back stalls. It took me a while to believe that I was good enough to play at this level.'

FORTY-ONE RUNS FROM SIX BALLS

Heidelberg roof-tiler Leigh Gray struck 41 runs from a six-ball over at James Reserve, home of the Banksia

Cricket Club in Melbourne, in 2001–02. Chasing Rosanna's 150, Banksia was 6/130 when Gray ended the game, striking a leg-spinner for 6 6 5 (a no-ball he hit for four) 6 6 6 6. The leggie's figures blew out from three for 40 from 17 overs to three for 81 from 18! Gray, 25, finished with 119 from 40 balls.

FOURTEEN BALLS IN AN OVER

George Tribe loved to attack a batsman, pinning him to the crease before looping a wrong 'un, wider and shorter, in the hope that he'd run down the wicket and miss it. Tribe particularly loved eight-ball overs, which he felt allowed a bowler to really work a batsman over.

Once, however, against Queensland, he bowled a 14-ball over – without once being no-balled. The umpire had clicked over his 8-ball counter just as George took a wicket.

'He thought he was at the start, rather than the end, of an over,' said long-time scorer Jack Cameron. 'Eventually, George said to him, "I reckon I've probably had enough now!"'

SEE: 'PUT TRIBE ON!', PAGE 162

FRAGILE JAKE

The first time Keith Miller took strike against Victoria's 'mystery' spinner Jack ('Jake') Iverson, he had no idea which way he was turning.

'We played Jake in Sydney and he bamboozled me and quite a few others [from NSW], too,' Miller said. 'I'd never faced him before in my life. He had a leg-break action and the ball darted back like an off-break. He did me completely the first couple of deliveries.'

But NSW's top six that summer were stronger than the visiting Englishmen and, after his initial successes against Miller, in at No. 3, Iverson lost his line and length, conceding more than 100 runs for the first time all summer.

'He pitched one outside my leg stump and I hit it for six,' said Miller, 'and told him he was a silly bastard to bowl there. We really hopped into him [Miller making 83 and Arthur Morris 182] and he didn't front up against us again. He said he was crook and couldn't play. But the truth was that he wasn't satisfied with his form. He hardly played another match for Victoria after that.'

A FRIENDLY RIVALRY

The West Indians were at a cocktail reception in Melbourne (1960–61) and someone was talking to Rohan Kanhai about his teammate, Garry Sobers.

'He must be a very great batsman,' said the admirer.

'You haven't seen *me* yet,' said Kanhai, grimly.

Kanhai made 252, one of the greatest innings at the MCG.

FRUIT FLY

Merv Hughes didn't go past year 10 at school; the teachers complained that not only was he a menace, he was downright dangerous – especially if let loose in the science lab.

Hughes also struggled for recognition as a cricketer, especially when he averaged 123 with the ball, made a duck, and was accused of drinking far more than a mountain of soda water on the eve of a forgettable debut. He was dropped after his first Test, and axed again after his second and sixth. He seriously debated hanging out full-time with his mates from Werribee and forgetting all about big cricket.

Less than a month later, Hughes was Australia's new cult hero, having taken a hat-trick in Perth against the world champions, the West Indies. And his big-hearted displays in England in '89 and '93 were crucial in Australia's runaway wins.

Hughes' teammates called him 'Fruit Fly' – the great Australian pest. But they loved him for his enthusiasm and ability to make it happen, especially when the weather was hot and the wickets flat.

THE FUMBLE THAT COST A FLAG

It was the Victorian district cricket final at the MCG (March, 1937) and Bill Ponsford was the star of a Melbourne Cricket Club team dominated by first-class and Test cricketers. But Richmond had a plan to dismiss the record-breaking Ponsford. Ernie McCormick was going to bounce him and the team's star outfielder, baseballer Charlie Stuckey, would take the catch on the backward square-leg fence.

'We had him in the exact spot,' said McCormick, 'right on the old practice wickets. And Ponny duly hooked and hit it straight down Charlie's throat, only for him to momentarily lose his footing on the slope near the fence, and down it went. It was early in Ponny's innings, too. We would have bolted it in but for that. He got 100 and they passed us eight-down. And they had an all-star team, too – guys like Ponny, Hans Ebeling, Fleetwood, Lyle Nagel, Keith Rigg and Percy Beames. But that's cricket, isn't it!'

GAME, SET AND MATCH

Dean Jones's famed self-confidence was frozen, temporarily, by Richard Hadlee in 1987–88, when the great New Zealander dismissed him three times in three matches – including once in front of his adoring home crowd in Melbourne in the Christmas Test. Jones had made just four when Hadlee delivered a searing throat-ball that Jones only just flicked away from his face. The next was a lifting leg-cutter that missed everything, followed by the pièce de résistance, a slower Hadlee outswinger, which Jones tried to drive, only to edge behind.

Jones made scores of 2, 38 not out, 0, 4 and 8. He was never again to regularly command the prized No. 3 batting position, which it had been assumed would remain his for years after his gutsy double-century against India just 15 months before. He also lost a substantial side-bet to New Zealand's Martin Crowe on who would make more runs during the Tests.

GARTH THE GREAT

'Great players are few, champions are rare,' said Bill Lawry. 'Graham McKenzie, both on and off the cricket field, must rate as an all-time champion. He was a captain's dream . . . never refusing to bowl, never limping when things were tough. He was the complete team player.'

Nicknamed 'Garth' after the strapping comic-book hero of the time, McKenzie led the Australian attack throughout the sixties, being at his absolute best on the tour of England in 1964, in South Africa in 1966–67, and in the opening Tests of the 1967–68 home season against India.

A humble and modest champion, McKenzie's big-hearted displays saw him dismiss the biggest names in the game. Throughout his reign, he maintained his popularity and image as one of the nice guys of world cricket.

Few were as superbly fit as McKenzie, or as capable of bowling extended spells on even the hottest of days. His bounce surprised many, with first slipsman Bob Simpson commenting that edged catches flew as fast from McKenzie's bowling as from anyone in his time.

GEMS FROM NUGGET (I)

Before charismatic Keith 'Nugget' Miller became one of Australia's ultimate Test cricket heroes, he was also an exceptional Aussie Rules footballer – good enough to hold the legendary Bob Pratt to just one goal in an important match. Nugget was 20 when he played his first League game for St Kilda at the old Junction Oval, mid-1940.

'I was virtually just out of school [Melbourne High], and lined up on a half-back flank against a fella called Ron 'Socks' Cooper, a West Australian who was a big name at the time at Carlton,' said Miller. 'You can imagine how pleased and excited I was. My first game. A good crowd in. I was really going to get amongst it. Just as the ball was being bounced, Socks glanced at me and went *bang* and down I went. He taught me more in a second or two than I would have learnt in 12 months.

'In my second game, I lined up on Ambrose Palmer, the champion boxer [then playing at Footscray]. What am I in for here?, I thought to myself. But he was a thorough gentleman . . . to me, anyway!

'Funnily enough, in my first game back after the War

[1946], I was playing against Syddy Dyer from North Melbourne and he kept trying to trip me. Finally, after another deliberate ankle tap, I'd had enough and I said, "Look Syd, in the War we were taught how to kill. Do you want me to revert?"

'He didn't go near me for the rest of the game!'

GEMS FROM NUGGET (II)

Richie Benaud told Miller one day how disappointed he was not to bowl to Don Bradman, who retired the very season Richie debuted. 'Son,' said Nugget, 'that was your *good* luck!'

GEMS FROM NUGGET (III)

New South Wales was playing Victoria on a greentop in Sydney. Miller tossed. Sam Loxton called tails . . . incorrectly.

'Sammy,' said Miller, 'what were you going to do if you won it?'

'Bat,' said Sam, without blinking an eyelid.

'You still bat,' said Miller.

The Vics were bowled out for 86 in two-and-a-half hours and lost in extra time on day two.

GEMS FROM NUGGET (IV)

Aside from having a bronze statue named in his honour (at the MCG, February, 2004), one accolade in particular made Miller merry. He says it was one of the few times he ever outdid Don Bradman.

'Both of us have our portrait at Lord's, but mine is in position A,' he said, 'right above the entrance to the public bar!'

Miller, the Errol Flynn of cricket, was just as revered

as the Don, and maybe even more loved – not only for his knockabout ways, charisma and sporting prowess, but for his distinguished war service in a series of daring bomber raids over Germany during his time in the RAAF. He was also a rascal, highly irreverent, and with the common touch – just as comfortable in the company of royalty as he was with his punting mates at Caulfield. His last, wheelchair-bound years were difficult, but he never lost his crop of hair or the twinkle in his eye.

We were neighbours on the Mornington Peninsula and he rang me one morning, very excited. He'd been watching Andrew Denton's interview with Michael Parkinson on *Enough Rope* the night before.

'Do you know what, Ken?' he said. 'Of all the film stars and personalities and world leaders that Parky has met and interviewed, do you know who he named as his all-time hero? Me! Little old Nugget.'

GENERAL'S GREATEST MOMENT

When John 'General' Grant took six for 37 against champions New South Wales (Sydney, February, 1966), not only was it a career-best performance, it ensured Victoria the Sheffield Shield. In what was a virtual play-off, long before the official finals were implemented, the last match of the summer was rain-ruined. Play didn't start until the fourth and final morning. Taking full advantage of the moist conditions, Grant bowled unchanged for two-and-a-half hours as NSW, led by ex-Test captain Brian Booth, was humbled for 93. The young Victorians took first innings spoils and the Shield.

'The touring team to New Zealand was being picked the following day,' said Grant, 'and the way it was written up the following morning, I thought I was a chance to go.

'I missed out, but it didn't take away any of the satisfaction we all felt in winning the title.'

With 29 wickets for the season, Grant, then 25, must have been in contention, given that it was a No. 2 Australian team being sent away, mainly for the experience. Two speedsters who did go, South Australians Eric Freeman and Alan Frost, were only slightly better-performed and Grant's batting was just as good, if not as explosive, as the big-hitting Freeman.

Grant says it was an honour even to break into Victoria's star-studded team, which was centred around its top five Australian representatives in captain Bill Lawry, Ian Redpath, Bob Cowper, Keith Stackpole and Paul Sheahan. To play 43 games and take more than 100 wickets in that powerful era was a bonus, he said.

'Even to get to that level was satisfying and as far as I could have expected to get, bearing in mind I was just 5'7" [168 cm]. To be perfectly honest, I wasn't that good. It was just my sheer determination, wanting to win and to play at the best possible level. I didn't want to die wondering.'

GENIAL, FEISTY, ANGRY CLEM HILL

Australia's first great left-hander, Clem Hill, was charming, popular and sunny-natured. His geniality was matched only by his considerable cricketing ability. One of an exclusive club of just 42 to captain Australia, Hill was also among the most even-tempered . . . that is, until his captaincy was questioned and he responded by punching a co-selector on the nose!

The resultant boardroom brawl in the offices of the NSW Cricket Association highlighted the rising bitterness in the power play between rebellious players and administrators. This struggle for control of the game bubbled into open warfare on the eve of the 1912 tour of England.

Hill never toured again. Nor, it's said, did he again speak to the selector he struck, East Melbourne's Peter McAlister.

'GET OFF, YA MUG – WE DIDN'T COME TO SEE *YOU*!'

Bruce Bowley was batting ahead of Don Bradman for Adelaide club team Kensington, only to be told by the large Saturday crowd, 'Get off the ground, ya mug – we didn't come to see *you*!'

Bowley, a regular South Australian Sheffield Shield representative, reckoned Bradman almost always protected the new batsman by taking most of the early bowling before, later, pacing himself.

'You went in and you wouldn't get strike for two or three overs,' he told author Margaret Geddes. 'He would take all the strike. He'd work in singles and whatever at the end of the over, and let you get used to the atmosphere. Then, as the day wore on, suddenly he'd have a period where he wouldn't have the strike. You'd have all the strike because he would have a rest and that, I believe, is one of the main reasons why he used to make such big scores.'

GETTING SERIOUS

Rosedale-Kilmany, down South Gippsland way, say they've never had a finer ring-in. Cameron Mayne, 32-year-old father of three, made 267 – including 14 sixes – against Heyfield (January, 2004). He'd been cajoled into playing again by his brother, Rohan, who captains the club's first XI.

'We were playing at Rosedale No. 2, which is a synthetic wicket,' said Mayne. 'Most went over midwicket. I've made four or five hundreds overall, including one in A-grade when I was 16, but nothing as big as that before. They put me up into B-grade after that, so I might try and play a few more games rather than just being a ring-in . . . I'm going to get a bit more serious about it.'

Fiji's left-arm fast bowler, A. Driu, claimed six wickets for the match in a light-hearted one-dayer against a NSW XI at the Sydney Cricket Ground in February 1960. The first Fijian team tour to Australia took place in 1907–08.

yours truly
Don Bradman

A young Don Bradman, soon after breaking into Australia's Test team.
INSET: The Bradman 'mask' of the early thirties, now a highly collectable piece of cricketing memorabilia.

Arthur Morris at net practice in Melbourne, as featured on a Coles swap card of the early fifties.

Bill Brown was ranked with Don Bradman as Australia's outstanding batsman during the 1938 tour of England.

A promotional poster for Clarrie Grimmett's book *Tricking the Batsman*, released in 1934. Known as 'Grum', Grimmett played into his late forties.

Keith Miller (second from the right) flanked by Lindsay Hassett and rookie Ian Craig early in the 1953 Coronation tour.

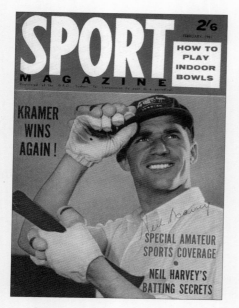

Among Australia's cricketers to enjoy front-page, flavour-of-the-month magazine status in the early fifties were 'Invincibles' Neil Harvey (left) and Bill Johnston.

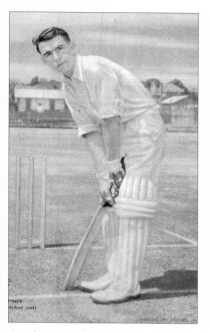

Aged 16, Bobby Simpson almost chose golf over cricket.

Mid-career, Norman O'Neill rejected a rich offer to play baseball for a living.

On the day Colin McDonald ensured a 4-0 Ashes victory for Australia in the fifth and final Test in Melbourne in February 1959, he received a telegram of congratulations from cricket-loving prime minister Sir Robert Menzies. McDonald made scores of 133 and 51 not out.

A mid-teens Shane Warne enjoying some R and R down the coast. Within years, he would be fast-tracked into state and Test cricket.

Ricky Ponting (right) won his first bat contract at 13; Adam Gilchrist opened the bowling in Scotland. Here, they pose with trophies in Auckland after Australia beat New Zealand by nine wickets to win the third and final Test in 2005.

Few practised as assiduously or as long as
Justin Langer. He was fair dinkum whether at
the nets – or on the beach at Antigua.
RAY TITUS/CRICKETER MAGAZINE

Glenn McGrath was first picked for
Australia directly out of the Australian Cricket
Academy in Adelaide. Here, he celebrates his
498th Test wicket in Auckland, 2005.
© REUTERS/ANTHONY PHELPS/PICTURE MEDIA

Adam Gilchrist is known for wearing his 'keeping gloves to the beach – as well as at the breakfast table!

SERGIO DIONISIO/AUSTRALIAN CRICKET MAGAZINE

A young champion in the making – Michael Clarke on making a century in his debut Test in Bangalore, 2004.

© REUTERS/ARKO DATTER/PICTURE MEDIA

GIFT OF THE GAB

You had to love Lindsay Hassett, cricket's little imp. At a team reception in a country town one day, he began his speech with, 'Never in my whole life have I seen a gathering of such ugly men!' Then, amidst the gasps, 'And never before have I seen so many gorgeous women.'

GOING DOWN LIKE FLIES

The Australians were going down like flies (Old Trafford, 1956) when tailender Ray Lindwall came in. Turning to England's wicketkeeper, Godrey Evans, he said, 'What's going on out here, Godfrey?'

'Can't understand it, Ray,' came the reply. 'Don't know why your fellows are getting out. There's nothing in it [the wicket].'

The first three balls Lindwall faced from Jim Laker (who took 19 wickets for the match) spun almost at right angles, one of them also beating Evans and going for four byes.

'Nothing in it, Godfrey?' Lindwall said to Evans.

'They're the first ones that have spun,' said Evans, with a huge grin on his face.

'Sure, Godfrey, sure . . .'

A GRAND OLD MAN

One of the hazards of playing into your fifties is that your body and reflexes invariably run a poor second behind your mind. The idea of a warm-up alongside kids less than a third of your age is preposterous. What was once a comfortable three to the foot of the backward square fence is now one, maybe two. And a turn at the crease is invariably nothing longer than an over, *after* the game is decided!

As a keen, once-competitive club cricketer now filling in just occasionally for my local team's third XI,

I've lost count of the cracks and quips reserved for me – from 'Let's give 'im somethin' to write about!' to 'C'mon lads, let's get Jimmy Olsen out . . .'

By far the best, however, came in the middle of one painfully slow knock where I'd struggled to hit the ball off the square and was puffing from the exertion of having to run two twos in a row.

'C'mon boys,' said the kid at point, 'let's get the grand old man out. The old people's home closes at five!'

SEE: 'MASTER, EVER THOUGHT ABOUT RETIRING?', PAGE 129

THE GRAND-DADDY OF THEM ALL

As tour larks go, this was the grand-daddy. But so compelling were the 500 to one odds that Dennis Lillee felt he just had to have a slice, even if it did mean betting *against* Australia. He put in £10, his mate Rod Marsh added £5 and, within 48 hours and courtesy of an astonishing English comeback, the pair had won £15 000 – enough to buy a double-fronter in inner Melbourne!

Ray Bright was rooming with Lillee and, walking into their Leeds hotel room that night, found the entire room littered with £1 and £5 notes.

'Dennis had won so much money they didn't have it in the tent,' Bright said. 'The rest was delivered the next day.'

A clause was soon inserted into official contracts forbidding players to bet on any game in which they were involved.

GRANDMA CONNIE SPOTS A STAR

No other Australian, not even Don Bradman, was given a bat contract at the age of 13. Ricky Ponting was in year 8 at Brooks High school in Launceston when he was approached by Kookaburra Sport representatives Rob Elliot and Ian Simpson.

'He was an exceptional player for his age, and was coming off four tons in four days in a schoolboy's competition in Launceston,' said Elliot. 'We felt if we didn't sign him, someone else would.'

Ponting's grandmother, Connie, had given him a T-shirt when he was aged four, complete with slogan, 'Inside this shirt is an Australian Test cricketer'. First selected for Tasmania as a 17-year-old, Ponting always had talent and a sophisticated understanding of the game. Rod Marsh proclaimed him the most exciting teenage batsman he'd ever seen during his two-year stint at the Commonwealth Bank Cricket Academy in Adelaide.

THE GREAT ESCAPE

It was a Test match Australia should never have won. But, thanks to some brilliant strategy and some gloriously uninhibited batting from the wonder-boy Neil Harvey, South Africa was beaten by five wickets in Durban (1949–50), despite having bowled the Australians out for just 75 in their first innings.

'It was an old-fashioned sticky wicket, a real shocker, ideal for a bowler like Hughie Tayfield,' said another of Australia's heroes, Sam Loxton. 'He cleaned us up, taking seven for 23. We should have lost easily, but [South Africa's captain] Dudley Nourse refused to enforce the follow-on.

'We started at them again with big Bill Johnston under instructions from [captain] Lindsay [Hassett] not to get anyone out, no matter what. He went through all the motions of turning the ball at right angles, but every one went straight. We were playing for time, not wanting to give the opposition an inkling of what the pitch was really like. Despite our best efforts, we got them out for 90-odd, and then we were set 336 on a wicket still playing tricks.

'I got 50-odd, but that paled into insignificance compared with Harv's hand. It was one of those flowing hands you dream about playing. It was an absolutely amazing performance.

'It's pretty hard to say which was Neil's greatest innings. His 112 at Leeds [1948] was magnificent, but his 151 not out this day – especially against Tayfield in the form he was in – just about takes the cake. There haven't been too many better off-spinners in the history of the game.'

SEE: 'WHO LEADS YOU OUT TO BAT?', PAGE 226

GREEN SHOOTS IN HIGH SUMMER

When the north wind blows through Melbourne in high summer, everything dries like parchment – from gardens and lawns to complexions and, in particular, cricket wickets.

In the 1954–55 Test, the cracks in the MCG's wicket were so wide that Arthur Morris reckoned it was fortunate Lindsay Hassett had retired – otherwise he would have been in danger of disappearing altogether!

However, curator Jack House flaunted the laws and watered the wicket on the Sunday, a day off for the players. On Monday morning, little green shoots greeted the players.

'We couldn't believe it,' said Morris. 'I went out with [Australia's captain] Ian Johnson to have a look. All the cracks had suddenly come together. The academics reckoned there was a subterranean river underneath the MCG; the heat had drawn up the moisture and greened up the wicket. But laymen like ourselves knew that the curator had watered it. It was like a brand new wicket all over again, and this was day three!

'Fortunately for the game, England batted most of that

day. Had Australia been batting, the English press would have called Australia the biggest cheats of all time.'

Set 240 to win late the following day, the Australians started well enough, reaching 1/57, only to be skittled when the great Englishman Frank 'Typhoon' Tyson took seven for 27 in the most lethal spell by an Englishman since Bodyline. Australia was out for just 111 in the highlight match of the series, as Len Hutton's Englishmen successfully defended the Ashes.

GREG CHAPPELL'S FIRST TEST

Tall, slim and athletic, Greg Chappell was the first Australian to make 7000 Test runs. From the early seventies until his retirement in 1984, he was widely acclaimed as the game's outstanding batsman. One of three brothers to play for Australia, two of whom emulated their grandfather Vic Richardson and captained their country, Chappell was a superb strokemaker. From the time he made a superb century from No. 7, on debut against England in the inaugural Test match in Perth in 1970–71, Chappell delighted purists with his composure and riveting array of shots.

'I went through the whole of the first Test match in a bit of a daze, really,' he said. 'I'd dreamed about playing Test cricket all through my childhood, but didn't really believe it would happen. It was more of a pipe dream than anything else.

'I'd played against most of the English bowlers for a couple of seasons with Somerset, and had seen them all before. And, as the seventh specialist batsman in that team, there weren't as many expectations from anyone. We were 5/107 when I went in [in Perth]. They concentrated their efforts on Ian Redpath, who was the senior player and not out at the other end.

'John Snow was their major strike bowler, but I don't think I faced him once in the first hour I was at the crease.

Red soaked up most of Snowy in that period. Whether it was by design or accident, he protected me and it was my good fortune.

'I'm told it took me 40 minutes to get off the mark, but it was a tense period of the game. They were on top. We had to stop them from taking more wickets.'

With 171, Redpath top-scored in the drawn match. He shared a memorable double-century stand with Chappell, who made 108 in a thrilling debut, his leg-side placements a feature.

GREIGY ON WORLD SERIES CRICKET

One of the key and most controversial signings for Kerry Packer's breakaways in 1977 was England captain Tony Greig.

'I wouldn't change my decision [to sign with World Series],' he said. 'My wellbeing, and that of my family, was most important. I may have been captain of England but, as my dear father reminded me, there had been many captains and, despite what they may have thought at the time, they didn't stay in the job forever.

'I was 32, I loved Australia and had a decision to make: Do I go back to South Africa [where he was born and bred]? Do I go to Australia? Where do I bring up my kids? We came here [Australia] and have never regretted it.

'In hindsight, just about the only thing I would have changed was the clandestine manner in which we all agreed . . . It was part of the strategy. The bottom line was that I went to work for someone else, just like occurs every day of the year elsewhere. It was a matter of saying, "Thanks for the ride. It was great. Now it's time to move on." And I did.'

h
||||||||||||

HE BOWLED WITHOUT SOCKS

It wasn't until Ian Johnson went on the Invincibles tour of 1948 that he reverted to wearing socks, having done without them in the warmer climate down-under for back-to-back Test tours in 1946–47 and 1947–48. According to author Mark Browning, Johnson's feet were hardened from wearing boots without socks during his flying days with the RAAF.

'In the [Pacific] Islands and New Guinea, foot ailments like tinea were a continual problem,' Johnson said. 'Wearing socks in that climate tended to make your feet sweaty and more susceptible to that sort of ailment, so I learned to do without them.

'When I returned home to play cricket, I was still used to not putting on socks. It was quite comfortable just going around in boots and I didn't change the habit until I went to England in 1948, where the cold weather demanded the use of socks – the thicker the better!'

HE CAPTAINED AUSTRALIA –
FOR EIGHT HOURS!

'You win some, you lose some,' says Bill Brown of his eight-and-a-half-hour tenure as captain of Australia's Test team. One of only 42 to captain Australia in 125 years of international cricket, Brown says he was grateful to have even two days at the helm.

The match he captained, in Wellington, had not even

been given official Test status at the time; that wasn't forthcoming for another two years.

'Don Bradman was still to come back after the War and, when we went to England after that, Lindsay Hassett was made vice-captain. There was no question on who'd be captain. That was Don,' said Brown.

'Lindsay was an excellent man. He captained the Services team [to England in 1945] . . . He was also younger.' (Brown was rising 34 and, he says, in his twilight years by 1945–46.)

While Brown's Test captaincy tenure, before Bradman's return, was the shortest in Australian history, Brown says the five-match tour, including the Wellington Test, was an incredibly happy one. The players were grateful to be involved in cricket again after the black years of war.

The opportunity to return to New Zealand for a reunion 50 years later remains one of the happiest of all Brown's cricket memories.

'HE COULD BAT A BIT!'

Sam Loxton had visions of joining the very select list of bowlers to dismiss the legendary Don Bradman when he opposed him for the first time, shortly after the War.

'We were in Adelaide, and I was first change after Billy Johnston and Freddy Freer, and very keen to get at him,' Loxton said. 'I pitched one on middle and leg just short of a length, and could almost see it straightening and piercing the great man's defences. But instead of the ball hitting the stumps, [Bradman] whipped it to the leg-side fence! As he was jogging up the wicket, I said to him, "That was a pretty good ball."'

'Ah Sammy,' Bradman replied, 'but a better shot.'

'He made 100,' Loxton remembers. 'It was chanceless, too. Yes, he could bat a bit!'

HE READ HIS OWN OBITUARIES

So seriously ill was popular ex-Testman Neil Hawke in the early eighties that his journalistic mates in Adelaide wrote his obituary. Since bowel surgery in 1980, Hawke's once-powerful body had shut down so comprehensively that his heart stopping beating 24 times. His system would not accept blood transfusions and he had to be drip-fed for almost two years. Candles were lit for him around the world and pilgrims brought water from Lourdes to his bedside.

Just as doctors were quietly advocating that Hawke's life-support system be turned off, his wife Beverley insisted that he return home, where his open wounds miraculously began to heal. He simply refused to die, and took great delight in reading and dissecting the obituaries his mates had prepared.

One Test match night in Adelaide, Freddie Trueman and a fleet of cricket identities came around, sharing tall stories and true. 'Hawkeye' was in his element. Every extra day was a bonus for him. He remains one of South Australia's foremost sporting heroes – and certainly the most courageous.

Hawke died on Christmas Day, 2000, aged 61 – almost 20 years after his initial surgery.

HE WON ALL ELEVEN TOSSES

Matty Duff, captain–coach of Frankston East in Victoria's Mornington Peninsula Cricket Association, played 11 matches and won all 11 tosses in 2002–03. He varied his call, and would call the opposite to whatever side the coin was facing before it was tossed. By the last game, and with Frankston East well out of finals contention, 11 beers were on offer should he win it again. Team-mates watched on expectantly and, to their cheers, Duff maintained his perfect record, making it 11 from 11.

Having elected to bat in the first eight games, of which just two were won, he began to insert the opposition – 'for something different' – but without greatly altering his team's losing ways.

Frankston East's second XI captain, Powell 'Pinky' Cooper, also won his first six tosses that summer.

HE WOULD HAVE BOWLED BODYLINE

Harry 'Bull' Alexander would gladly have retaliated and bowled bodyline in his one-off Test against England in Sydney (1932–33), but for captain Bill Woodfull's insistence that the Australians not be involved.

'Woody even refused to allow me to have a square leg,' said Alexander. 'For most of the time, I had only a mid-on and a fine leg.'

Alexander was sharp enough to smack the reviled Douglas Jardine on the calf. He also split Jardine's fingers and broke two of vice-captain Bob Wyatt's bats.

At 182 cm (just over six feet), Alexander was Harold Larwood's height and, at his fastest, was near express. He'd won acclaim as a player of genuine talent in 1928–29, when he twice dismissed the world's No. 1 batsman, Walter Hammond, in only his second match against the MCC. Cricket writer Ray Robinson said his short deliveries against Jardine were applauded by sections of the Sydney crowd, such was the resentment built up by Bodyline.

'I still regard that [Test] as the best I ever bowled,' said Alexander. He claimed that five catches were dropped off his bowling, on his way to match figures of 1/154.

'I was always a bit sore that I wasn't allowed at least a square leg. Yet everyone expected me to bump them down. I wasn't in the race without a couple of extra men on the leg-side.'

'HE'S OUT . . . HE'S OUT'

Eric Freeman was at short leg, in the 1968–69 Christmas Test in Melbourne, when the West Indian Seymour Nurse pulled a ball from mystery spinner John Gleeson on to Freeman's unprotected forehead. It glanced off his head and was taken by Keith Stackpole at midwicket.

'I was pretty lucky, as the ball only just missed my temple,' said Freeman. 'I used to love fielding at short leg. I'd watch the batsman and, when you saw him go to sweep, pull or hook, you'd turn your body. It hit me flush on the head. I knew it had deflected and next minute I heard Barry Jarman, the wicketkeeper, saying, 'He's out . . . he's out'.

'I remember thinking to myself, "Yeah, I'm out all right . . . I'm on the ground!" I went off for a while and had a headache for a couple of days but, other than that, there was no damage.'

HEADINGLEY HEROICS

For all his finest centuries at Test level, Steve Waugh says none compares with his 120 not out in a one-day international at Headingley. In the famous run chase, Australia was set a formidable 272, and won with two balls to spare. The match saved Waugh's captaincy and lifted Australia into the 1999 World Cup semifinals.

Mid-innings, Herschelle Gibbs dropped Waugh. The catch, at midwicket, was simple, but Gibbs attempted to throw it skywards in celebration before (according to the umpires) he had controlled it. At the change of overs, the super-competitive Waugh asked Gibbs, 'How does it feel to have tossed away the match?' (Waugh insists he said 'match' rather than 'World Cup', which is still widely reported.)

Had Australia not qualified through to the semifinals,

Waugh said he would almost certainly have been stood down as captain after the most chequered of campaigns. Instead, he was to pilot a wonderful run of consecutive Test victories, during which the Australian team won a record 16 matches in a row.

THE HEAT IS ON

Tom Graveney was 44 in 1969, and well past his best, when cajoled into playing several seasons with Queensland.

'I'd come over purely to coach, but Clem Jones [Queensland's cricketing supremo] said, "You will play," so I did.

'I did have one good innings, in a semifinal of the Coca-Cola Cup in Adelaide, when I got 90-odd – and against a team that included the Chappells, Barry Richards and Terry Jenner,' Graveney said.

'It was very hot living in Queensland. Often we played in 100-degree [Fahrenheit] heat. The humidity was very high, too. In those days they didn't have a very good side and, if we won the toss, we'd invariably put the opposition in. After a day and a half in the field, I was gone.'

HELLO AND GOODBYE

No one made a finer hello and goodbye to Test cricket than Bill Ponsford, the mega run-scorer famous for saying, 'By cripes, I'm unlucky' after a ball ricocheted from his boot and broke his stumps one day in Melbourne. He'd made 352! A scorer of centuries in each of his first two Ashes Test matches, as well as a double in his last, Ponsford was the ultimate record-breaker, and still the only Australian to make two 400-plus scores, both at his beloved MCG.

Ponsford died in 1991 and it was fitting, at the start of the 2004–05 summer, that the MCG's rebuilt western stand was once again named in his honour. His sons – Bill jnr, 75, and Geoff, 72 – were among generations of family members to attend the unveiling. They spoke fondly of their father, who'd use cricket stumps as incinerator pokers and Australian blazers as extra insulation for his dogs at night.

'He loved his bowls and, in particular, his fishing,' said Bill Jr. 'We had a 16-footer, which Dad would take out [off Rosebud] during the school holidays. We all got a lot of pleasure from it and caught all sorts of things, from whiting to nice-size snapper.

'He was a patient batsman and, in many ways, he got that from his fishing expeditions. He was happy to sit and wait and smoke his pipe. He was a different kind of fisherman to Rex Hunt!

'He could be an autocratic captain, though. He'd stay up the back while we ran around doing all the work. One time, I was up the front, waiting to moor the boat at the jetty. Dad came in too quickly and I ended up in the drink! It saved me having to have a shower that night. They were happy days, and we would stay there with Mum even when Dad went back to work [as the office manager at the Melbourne Cricket Club].'

In one of his last interviews, with Melbourne writer Robert Coleman for his book *Seasons in the Sun*, Ponsford said the best part of his English tours were the boat trips there and back. 'They were much better than flying. You had time to get to know people,' he said.

SEE: BIG BERTHA, PAGE 20

'HERE'S YOUR THEATRE TICKETS, DOUGIE'

When Kerry Packer pirated the cream of the world's finest to form his rebel cricket troupe in 1977, it smashed the cricket establishment's monopoly, introduced exciting, entertaining innovations to a captive new television audience, and ushered in a fresh prosperity for the game.

In a masterstroke of bold, top-secret planning that changed the very dynamics of the age-old game, the world's best players signed contracts guaranteeing them the security they'd been denied for years. Establishment cricket was plunged into a bitter, 23-month conflict with Australia's richest man, who was hell-bent on obtaining exclusive rights for his television network.

The scandal also triggered some extraordinary moments. During the establishment's mega event, Melbourne's Centenary Test, World Series Cricket's Austin Robertson handed star signee Doug Walters an envelope containing a hefty sign-on advance. 'Here's your theatre tickets, Dougie,' Robertson said cheerfully.

'HEY MAN, YOU HIT MY BALL TOO HARD!'

Ian Sartori was a true Bradman of the bush in the nineties, amassing more runs and being selected in more all-Australian country cricket teams than anyone. Originally from Daylesford, he is now based at Katandra West, where he and his wife, Bronwyn, run the general store. Among his favourite memories are several international games, especially one against the West Indies when he was opposed to Patrick Patterson, then the fastest bowler in the world.

'They [the West Indians] didn't go too hard, but were still pretty bloody quick,' Sartori said. 'If you played a shot they didn't like, the next ball would be two yards quicker.

'We played them in Newcastle and almost 8000 showed up. I only made a handful, but really creamed one shot into the covers, and Keith Arthurton said, "Hey man, you hit my ball too hard!"'

HIS LUCKY DAY

St Kilda medium-pacer Glenn Lalor boasted a rare analysis of 1-1-0-4 in the Victorian Cricket Association's Premier League game against Hawthorn-Monash University at the Junction Oval in 2001–02. Chasing 139, the Hawks were 5/87 before losing their last five wickets for nil, with Lalor taking a hat-trick and four wickets in five balls. When he also won the team's Melbourne Cup sweep that day, teammates advised him to bypass the celebrations afterwards and go straight to a Tattslotto agency.

'HIS NAME IS DENNIS LILLEE . . .'

John Snow was at his intimidating best in 1970–71, when England regained the Ashes for the first time since 1956. Late in the summer and with Australia trailing, Sir Donald Bradman, Australia's selection chairman, asked co-selectors Neil Harvey and Sam Loxton if they'd seen any young fast bowlers around Australia capable of returning a little of Snow's fire.

'As a matter of fact, we have,' they said.
'Who?'
'His name is Dennis Lillee and he comes from Perth.'
Bradman hadn't seen Lillee, even on television, but bowed to their judgement. Lillee was to take 355 Test and 79 Supertest wickets, making him arguably the finest Australian fast bowler of the century.

HORSESHOE'S LUCKY STREAK

So upset was England captain Arthur Gilligan by the luck of his Australian counterpart Herbie Collins before the Adelaide Test of 1924–25 that he kicked Collins's gold sovereign into the back of the George Giffen Stand. Known as 'Horseshoe Herbie', Collins won four of five tosses that summer. He was a bookmaker by profession.

AUSTRALIANS TO WIN ALL FIVE TOSSES IN A SERIES
M. A. 'Monty' Noble, v. England, 1909
A. L. (Lindsay) Hassett, v. England, 1953

SEE: JACKO'S TIMELY SIDESTEP, PAGE 109

HOTSPOT

Such was the chaos and confusion that only a few noticed Greg Chappell leading his Australian players off the WACA Ground. Perth's Black Saturday (November 13, 1982) has never been forgotten by the cricket fraternity – particularly Terry Alderman, who was struck from behind by an on-field assailant.

The commotion had started when a dozen spectators, carrying a Union Jack flag, jumped the fence late on Saturday and ran on to the field to celebrate England's 400. Fielding close to the boundary in front of the scoreboard, Alderman was struck from behind and, as he chased and brought down his attacker, he fell awkwardly on his shoulder and lay in agony. Dennis Lillee headlocked the man while his teammates frantically signalled for help. Clutching a dislocated shoulder, which was to sideline him from international cricket for almost 18 months, Alderman was carried from the field on a stretcher while police fought with dozens of fans who had jumped the fence.

Only 12 policemen were on duty and they were

hopelessly outnumbered. One policeman was knocked unconscious. It wasn't until reinforcements arrived that peace was restored and, after a 15-minute delay, the game resumed.

Black Saturday was one of a brace of provocative incidents at the WACA during the late seventies and early eighties. From the Lillee aluminium bat uproar, during the 1979–80 Ashes summer, through to the Lillee/Javed Miandad kicking incident, four years later, the WACA was a Test cricketing hotspot.

HUMBLE BEGINNINGS (I)

Twins Steve and Mark Waugh were seven when they played their first cricket match. Mark was clean-bowled by the first ball he faced. Steve blocked one before being bowled by the second, and their team was all out for nine. Not knowing what a protective box was for, Steve put it on his knee and strapped his pad over it. He still recalls the incident as his most embarrassing early memory of cricket.

HUMBLE BEGINNINGS (II)

When Neil Harvey first played for Victoria, he didn't have his own equipment. Everything was borrowed from the Victorian Cricket Association's kit.

'Even when I played for the first time [for Australia], against India in 1947–48 in Adelaide, I still didn't have any gear,' Harvey said. 'I'd saved up a little bit of pocket money Mum had given me and, with this money, I went down to the MSD [Melbourne Sports Depot] and bought myself a brand new Gunn & Moore cricket bat. I took that bat to Adelaide and within two overs the handle broke! Along with my borrowed pads and gloves, I had to borrow a bat to finish my innings.

'In the following Test against India, this time in Melbourne, I had to borrow the old gear again and, with a borrowed bat, I made 153. Cricketers today are spoilt rotten . . .'

HUMMING 'EM DOWN

Wicketkeeper Bert Oldfield was past his fortieth birthday and having trouble picking the wrist-spin of first-time tourist Chuck Fleetwood-Smith (South Africa, 1935).

'You'll have to give me a signal for the wrong 'un, Chuck,' said Oldfield. 'I can't pick it.'

'Don't worry about signals,' said Fleetwood-Smith. 'Just listen for it . . . It [the wrong 'un] makes more noise coming through the air.'

SEE: THE FIRST 'BALL OF THE CENTURY', PAGE 74

i

|||||||||||||

'I GOING NOW!'

During the first World Cup in 1975, diminutive Sri Lankan opener Sidath Wettimuny had his big toe crushed twice in the same over by Australia's expressman, Jeff Thomson. Despite urgings from his teammates, Wettimuny refused to go off. Shortly afterwards, it happened a third time and he said, 'I going now!' before literally jumping on a stretcher.

IF HE COULD TURN BACK TIME (I)

It's dangerous to flag your intentions to retire. Just ask Bobby Simpson, who succeeded Richie Benaud as Australia's captain in 1963.

'I gave the selectors notice in '67 so Bill [Lawry] could get some experience,' said Simpson, 'and they promptly dropped me – even though I'd made centuries in the previous two Tests.'

IF HE COULD TURN BACK TIME (II)

Australian all-rounder Tom Veivers can laugh about it now. But at the time, he was in trouble . . . big trouble. As many kids do, he'd hammer in the stumps with the face of the bat and think little of the damage it was causing.

One afternoon, he was given an old-looking bat by one of his uncles. Keen for a game, he set up the stumps and bashed them in with the face, as usual. It wasn't until his father realised what all the hammering was about that Tom wished he hadn't.

'I got a hiding,' Veivers said, 'and one I've never forgotten. Because the bat was from the '36–'37 Ashes series and had the signatures of both the Australian and the English players on it, including Don Bradman!'

IN GRAND COMPANY

Andy Bichel has something in common with Garry Sobers, Ravi Shastri and one or two others: they all hit 36 runs in an over. Batting for Cambridgeshire club Milton against Roses in 1992, Bichel made 194 not out from just 153 balls, including six sixes in a row from the final over (bowled by a gent called Davies).

IN PRIVATE

'That's Keith for you – he gets all the women in!' said Peg Miller, when word found its way back that her handsome husband, Keith, had had a private dinner with a youthful Princess Margaret at her uncle Lord Mountbatten's residence (England, 1956).

SEE: GEMS FROM NUGGET, PAGE 80

IN THE RIGHT PLACE AT THE WRONG TIME (I)

Scorer of more than 10 000 first-class runs, Sam Trimble was a victim of one of Australian cricket's most enduring opening partnerships, between Bill Lawry and Bobby Simpson in the sixties. Just like fellow Queenslander Jimmy Maher, who was the reserve opener behind Matthew Hayden and Justin Langer in the early years of the new millennium, Trimble was a top-notcher . . . but in the right place at the wrong time. Only once did he ever make an Australian XII, at Port of Spain in the final Test of the West Indian tour in 1964–65.

'I played for Australia, but not in any Tests. But I played a long time and made so many friends,' he said. 'The dollars weren't in it then.

'I was a bit unfortunate, I suppose. If you thought about it [not making an XI] you could be a little regretful. But I enjoyed the trip to the West Indies and made a lot of runs.

'While I was twelfth man in only one Test, I fielded in every match. We had only 15 in the team and there were always two or three away in hospital having X-rays! I batted as well as I could have batted over there, and made 101 in my only hit, before being hit on the thumb at St Kitts in the game between the first and second Tests. I kept playing, but had to bat mainly one-handed for a while after that.

'When I came back [to Australia], if I'd taken the advice, gone to Sydney and opened with Simmo [Bob Simpson], my chances may have been a little better. I felt isolated a bit up in Queensland. If I'd gone, Simmo and I would have been a pair. It could have made the difference.'

SEE: AUSTRALIAN TWELFTH MEN NEVER TO PLAY A TEST, PAGE 172

IN THE RIGHT PLACE AT THE WRONG TIME (II)

Geff Noblet just about touched the clouds when he bowled. At 188 cm (6'3"), he dwarfed almost all his teammates and, in a tour match in Adelaide (1951–52), dismissed the great West Indian Frank Worrell first ball in both innings.

Competition for international places was so intense, however, that he played just three Tests. In a fourth, as twelfth man (Melbourne, 1951–52), he ran for Arthur Morris in both innings after the left-hander injured his thigh in the field. Morris made only six and 12, but Noblet regarded it as a privilege to run for one of the finest batsmen he ever opposed.

INDIAN SUMMER

Left-handed Ken Eastwood was 35 when he had the summer of his life (1970–71), amassing almost 750 runs at an average of 90-plus to lift himself into the Test team. Included were scores of 201 not out and 177 against powerful New South Wales. His double-century at the SCG remains a particular favourite, as he was opposed to mystery spinner John Gleeson.

'Up until then, in the one or two meetings we'd had, he [Gleeson] had made me look a dill,' said Eastwood. 'Brian Taber was NSW's captain and, as soon as anyone came in who hadn't faced him before, he couldn't get Gleeson on quick enough.

'In this game, the wicket was pretty wet and we'd lost a couple of quick ones. They brought Gleeson on soon after lunch and he had bat-pads on both sides of the wicket. I played and missed a couple of times, and I walked down to Paul Sheahan, asking if he minded if I had a go. "Unless I do, I'm bound to get an edge [bringing the bat-pad catchers into play]," I told him.

'Paul agreed and I started sweeping the ball off middle stump. One edge carried over the top of slips. Another I hit sweetly, straight into Alan Turner's knee [at short leg]. They carried him off.

'Once you found out which way he [Gleeson] was going, it was a bit easier. You had to think in reverse, though. His back-of-the-hand delivery was an off-spinner to me [spinning in], and the front-of-the-hand one was his leg-spinner.'

Eastwood says it was a bonus to have played even one Test match. He'd missed selection in the opening three state games that summer, when Victoria's top six consisted of international quartet Bill Lawry, Keith Stackpole, Ian Redpath and Sheahan, plus prominent Sheffield Shield players John Scholes and Peter Bedford.

'IS THAT FOR YOU OR ME, MATE?'

On the eve of the Ashes Test in Melbourne in 2002, there was much speculation about Steve Waugh's immediate future and, as he walked in to bat in the nets on Christmas Eve, there was generous applause from hundreds of Melburnians camped behind the wickets. Justin Langer had also just walked in and was marking his guard in an adjoining net. Langer paused and, with a wide smile, called to Waugh, 'Is that for you or me, mate?'

Langer was to make centuries on both day one and day two of the Test. His 250 was a Test-best score.

'I'd watch Tugga [Waugh] prepare for a Test match and he'd always hit a lot of balls,' said Langer. 'He'd always said preparation was the key: do your hard work in the nets and enjoy the actual batting [in the middle]. That net session on Christmas Eve was important to how I batted in the Test. I hit everything in the middle. And it gave me a lift going into the match.'

'IT'S BIG, ISN'T IT?'

Greg Matthews was bowling to Simon O'Donnell at the MCG when O'Donnell, then captaining Victoria, launched a straight drive with such awesome authority and timing that Matthews didn't dare look.

'It's big, isn't it?' he said to O'Donnell, as the ball disappeared 100 metres and more into the second deck of the newly built Great Southern Stand.

IVERSON'S UNDERARM

Trevor Chappell's infamous underarm was not the only one bowled by an Australian at international level postwar. Jack Iverson bowled one during the Commonwealth tour of India in 1953–54, after an opposing No. 11 repeatedly played at and missed his mystery spinners. Sam Loxton was at silly mid-on. He said Iverson had made the tailender look foolish with his overarms, and thought he might finish him off completely with a sharply spun underarm.

Loxton remembers Iverson saying to the umpire, 'Mr Umpire, I desire to bowl underarm, right-hand from here, over the wicket.'

'He used to do it in the dressing room for his and our amusement,' Loxton says of Iverson. 'And back he stepped, and lobbed this one up which the batsman had no idea about, and it lobbed meekly off the splice straight to me. I put it in my pocket and off we went. Game over.'

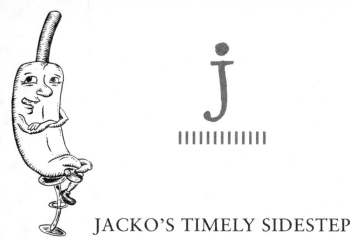

J

||||||||||||

JACKO'S TIMELY SIDESTEP

Thoroughly exasperated after losing all five tosses to England's F. S. Jackson during the 1905 Ashes series, Australian captain Joe Darling adopted a different tactic as the tour wound down with several light-hearted games at Scarborough. Stripping to the waist to reveal his powerful torso, Darling was ready to wrestle Jackson for the right to bat first.

'Now we'll have a proper tossing!' he said.

Jackson bypassed the challenge, instead calling for the swarthy George Hirst to take his place. Darling reluctantly agreed to toss in a more conventional manner – and promptly called incorrectly for the seventh time in a row!

SEE: HORSESHOE'S LUCKY STREAK, PAGE 99

A JEWELL IN THE CROWN

Nerida Jewell met her beau, Victorian cricketer Nick Jewell, at Gardenvale State School in suburban Melbourne.

'I was the older woman,' she says, 'two grades higher than him – and I couldn't stand him! He was one of those kids to be avoided at all costs!'

Their love blossomed years later, however, when she asked him to a social at Brighton Secondary College.

'I gave him a kiss and then ran off,' she said. 'He was on the phone the next day, inviting me out, and it went from there.'

The only bad habit Nerida would like Nick to change is his penchant for toenails. 'He chews them,' she said. 'It's disgusting.'

JOIN THE QUEUE

Each English winter, in between cricket seasons, Test umpire-to-be Bill Alley would happily go on the dole. He'd front up in the queue each week to collect his cheque, much of which was spent at his favourite local in Somerset.

The dole officer chided him one day, asking why he hadn't applied for a particular job. 'You mind your manners,' replied Bill, who was born and bred in Australia's Hawkesbury River region. 'It's blokes like me that keep you in a job!'

k

KANDY CAPERS

David Hookes made a habit of being the action attraction. The night he blasted his one and only century for Australia (Kandy, 1983), he lit a series of penny bungers and pushed them under the door of each of his teammates.

'It was past midnight and we thought the Australian team was subject to a terrorist attack,' said Graham Yallop. 'Everyone dashed into the corridor, in various states of undress, to see Hookesy doubled over with laughter, absolutely rapt with the success of it all.'

A 'KEEPER WHO COULD BOWL

One of the few wicketkeepers in my acquaintance who recognises that he *can't* bowl is Adam Gilchrist. After one embarrassing stint with the ball, as captain of the Prime Minister's XI, he declared he would never bowl again, even if they were short in the nets!

Bowling had run in the Gilchrist family, with Adam's grandfather, Bill, once taking 17 wickets in a match and his father, Stan, taking 15. Adam did open the bowling for Perthshire when he played in Scotland as a professional, but says he'd rather glove a new ball than bowl one.

One of the very best bowling 'keepers was the West Australian Tim Zoehrer who, later in his career, would regularly keep wickets while the ball was new, before doubling as West Australia's specialist spinner. After seeing Zoehrer claim seven wickets for the match with his wrist-spinners (against South Australia in Adelaide in 1991–92), ex-Test spinner Ashley Mallett declared in *Cricketer* magazine that 'Zoehrer had more natural ability as a leg-spinner than any I have seen on the first-class scene for many years . . . The South Australian batsmen were totally at sea trying to fathom his flight and turn.' Included in Zoehrer's haul was the celebrated David Hookes, twice.

Season 1991–92 was Shane Warne's first as an international player. Before seeing Warne play in a first-class match, Mallett wrote, 'I have seen Warne in the nets and he appears to have it all: the leg-break, toppy, wrong 'un, and he gives it a big tweak. I haven't seen him excel in a match, but I have seen Zoehrer. And right now, Zoehrer is the one to write home about.'

During the '93 Ashes tour, Zoehrer headed the averages with 12 wickets at an average of 20, including a best performance of three for 16 against the Combined Universities at Oxford. He was a member of the Australian XI that tied the second Test against India at Madras in 1986–87.

KEEPING MUM

The weekend before Doug Ring was due to represent Australia for the first time (Melbourne, 1947–48), he was bitten on his right thumb by a spider while opening his gate.

'My thumb soon swelled to twice its normal size,' Ring said, 'and there was only a few days to go before the game. I wasn't going to tell anybody. I had no idea if I was ever going to get the chance to play again.'

Having trained with Richmond Football Club to keep fit during the winter, Ring contacted the club's doctor, who was able to reduce the swelling so he could at least move the thumb.

'I made sure I didn't have a bat in the nets the day before, and I found I could bowl without my thumb. It was quite eventful at the time.'

The game, against first-time tourists India, was a glorified selection trial, with Queensland's Len Johnson and another Victorian, Sam Loxton, also included for the first time. By taking six wickets for the game, including three for 17 as India was bowled out a second time for just 67, 28-year-old Ring ensured his place on the celebrated 1948 tour, Don Bradman's last to England.

KING OF THE NIGHTWATCHMEN

Winemaker Tony 'Rocket' Mann is best known for scoring a century as a nightwatchman against Bishen Bedi's 1977–78 Indians in his home town of Perth. It was something he'd done before – and against an international touring side – seven years earlier. Sent in at No. 3 against the visiting MCC, Mann scored the fastest century of the season, from just 92 balls. Of his 110 runs, 64 came in boundary hits.

'I liked to play my game and go after the bowling,' he said. 'The week before I made the ton against the Indians, I'd got 50 or 60 against them for WA. I spent a lifetime bowling [leg-spinners] on the WACA and it didn't spin much, and the Indian attack revolved almost entirely around spinners, so I was confident of doing well.

'I thought I was a bit unlucky to get out, actually. The ball came from my bat on to my boot and ballooned up in front of me, allowing the keeper, Syed Kirmani, time to come around and dive and take it. It was a brilliant catch.'

Mann's 105 helped Australia to run down 342 in the fourth innings – still among the top six chases in Australian Test history.

LADY LUCK

The best part of Ian Quick's trip to England in 1961 was that he met his wife, Cora, at a reception in Northampton. Other than one appearance as twelfth man in the famous Manchester Test, Quick said he was never in serious contention for a place in the team and, on his return, was to play only once more for Victoria before business commitments took priority. By 1963, he had retired altogether.

'Cora and I had been introduced at a team reception. But we probably wouldn't have seen each other again, except that Ford [his employer in Geelong] sent me back just after Christmas that same year,' Quick said.

Quick believed he'd won a place in the touring 17 simply because there was no other finger-spinner, other than West Australia's Keith Slater, in direct contention. Quick had been the leading wicket-taker on the Australian B-team tour of New Zealand 12 months earlier. On his touring debut, against Auckland, his figures included seven for 20 and five for 78. Quick said his five wickets in the match for an Australian XI against a combined XI in Launceston on the eve of the Ashes team announcement had been crucial.

'Don Bradman [then Australia's selection chairman] was at that game and he congratulated me from the other side of the dressing-room. Earlier that summer, I thought I was lucky to be keeping my place in the Victorian side. Until that '61 tour, games had been played on uncovered

wickets [only the run-ups being covered] and, tradition-
ally, Australia had always taken a left-arm finger-spinner.
You needed one for the wet wickets.

'I was lucky to be there. We were just amateurs. Half
the side worked for cigarette companies, purely because
it was the only work they could get. I was an engineer and
was fortunate to get the time off to play. With boat travel
either way, the English tour went for nine or ten months.
It was a long time to be away from home. Today they are
all professionals and you can't have a separate, specialist
career.'

Quick, 188 cm (6'3"), had started his career at Corio
as a wrist-spinner, before changing to finger-spin after
the success of the West Indian Alf Valentine in 1951–52.
He developed subtle pace changes but said he offered too
many loose balls, of which the good batsmen took full
advantage. He particularly enjoyed bowling at the MCG,
where the bounce could be variable, and he struck quite
an understanding with wicketkeeper Len Maddocks.

THE LAST STAND

When Australia's No. 11, Lindsay Kline, walked down
the member's steps and on to the Adelaide Oval in 1960–
61, there were still 109 minutes to play. A West Indian
victory seemed certain.

'It probably didn't help when news of my form in the
practice nets half an hour earlier got back to the boys,'
Kline said. 'Johnny Martin and Normie O'Neill were
bowling to me and I reckon they bowled me 10 or 12
times. There was one woman watching on and she said
it was a waste of time me going out to face Wes Hall and
the rest of them.

'There didn't seem to be much more confidence in our
dressing-room, either, as the boys were all packing their
bags. There were no parting instructions as I walked

out, but Slasher [Ken Mackay] did say that I could bat better than most thought and, if I concentrated on every ball, we could keep them out there for a while.

'I took his advice, and suddenly there was only about 40 minutes to go. That's when I started to tense up, realising that a draw was a genuine option. Slasher camped himself at one end, taking Wes Hall – including [Hall's] epic last over, when [Slasher] allowed the last one to crash into his ribs. He figured that was safer than playing the ball.

'Our rooms were ecstatic and the West Indies, as disappointed as they were, still came in to congratulate us.'

Kline and Mackay added 66 for the last wicket, the second-biggest stand of the innings. Mackay finished with 62 not out and Kline with 15 – one of the few batting highlights of his career, which saw him average 8.28 for Australia, 8.97 for Victoria and 13.81 for Melbourne.

Had a Mackay catch, close in, not been disallowed by umpire Col Egar, the West Indies would have won with 90 minutes to play and taken a 2–1 lead, with the deciding Test in Melbourne still to be played.

LAUGHTER IS THE BEST MEDICINE (I)

Ernie McCormick had the happy knack of always seeing the lighter side. When no-balled 19 times in three overs at Worcester in Australia's opening game of the '38 tour, he told concerned teammates, 'It's all right, the umpire's hoarse!'

LAUGHTER IS THE BEST MEDICINE (II)

Before McCormick's first game with Richmond's first XI, old stager Les Keating stressed upon the teenager the importance of getting on with the umpires. He should always make a point of introducing himself, congratulating the umpires on their tidy appearance, and saying how much he was looking forward to being a part of the game they were umpiring, Keating told him.

'One time, there was a little gentleman umpiring his first district game,' said McCormick. 'He was done up like Ajax – brand new white coat, starched shirt, immaculate boots. I said to him, "Good afternoon, sir, and congratulations on your appointment to district cricket. Might I also compliment you, sir, on your attire?"

'In the first over, I think I got three leg-befores and, with my third appeal, he beat me by a split second!'

A LEGEND IN HIS OWN LUNCHTIME

Few in Australian cricket enjoy mealtimes quite like Jason 'Cheesie' Arnberger who, his teammates say, will blow out to the size of a block of flats as soon as he stops playing cricket. His mates reckon that when Arnie isn't training or running after his two young kids, he's flicking through the interstate *Yellow Pages*, planning his menus, trip by trip.

'He was inconsolable when Sizzler closed down in Brisbane,' said Jon Moss. 'He loved the $10 all-you-can-eat.

'Some of the smorgasbords up in the Dandenongs put out sentries on a Sunday, looking for Arnie's red Hyundai. They use walkie-talkies so they can get out their 'BOOKED OUT' signs – otherwise they reckon Arnie would eat a day's profits all in one sitting!

'Once on a roll, he's untouchable,' said Moss. 'You buy party pies three at a time after a game at Prahran and it's nothing for Arnie to munch his way through seconds and then thirds. Then he wants to know where we're going for tea!'

LIFE BEGINS AT FIFTY

Dennis Lillee was 50 when he played in his last meaningful match: a tour opener for the Chairman's XI against

Pakistan in 1999–2000. Opening the bowling alongside his son, Adam, he took three for 8.

Don Bradman played his last game at 55, when he came out of retirement to play for the Prime Minister's XI against the 1962–63 Englishmen. He made four.

Lindsay Hassett played charity games into his mid-fifties, while Leo O'Brien still appeared semi-regularly for the Melbourne Cricket Club's XXIXers at age 70.

SEE: OUTLAWED, PAGE 149

LIFETIME SCARS

It took Ian Meckiff more than 20 years to agree to play even social cricket after he was no-balled out of the game in December, 1963.

The first Saturday in summer is always painful for the slim South Melbourne expressman who, in the late fifties, bowled as fast as anyone in Australia. Called for throwing by Col Egar during his opening over of the Brisbane Test in 1963–64, Meckiff said the scars were long-lasting. He retired immediately – and didn't play again until the mid-eighties, when he joined in a social game at Ayers Rock. Ironically, Col Egar was umpire and called him again, on cue. This time there were smiles all round.

Asked why he hadn't continued, even at club level, when many – like Victoria's Test selector, Jack Ryder – were encouraging him to play on, Meckiff said, 'I felt if I had have played district cricket, I could have finished up with an umpire who might have wanted to get his name in the newspaper by calling me again. I wasn't ready for that. I'd gone through enough and my family had too. They were hurting just as much as me.'

A LITTLE STIFF FROM BOWLING

Arthur Mailey was a delightfully whimsical man-of-Redfern, known for lobbing his leg-breaks ever so high into the stratosphere. He always joked that his four for 362 – the most expensive figures in Australian first-class history – were greatly exaggerated, as a bloke in a trilby hat seated 20 rows back at midwicket had dropped the Victorian, Jack Ryder, three times during his six-laden 295!

A cartoonist and raconteur, Mailey was also a charming and witty companion, who was in his element on tour. He liked to describe a dinner dance at a stately home, south of London, to which the Australian team was invited. The hostess, a Lady Dash, was anxious for everyone to enjoy themselves.

'Aren't you dancing, Mr Mailey?' Lady Dash asked.

'No, Lady Dash,' he said. 'I'm a little stiff from bowling.'

'Oh,' she replied, 'so that's where you come from!'

SEE: RUNNING LATE, PAGE 176

LOOKING FOR COVER

Few matched the brutal strength of New Zealand all-rounder Lance Cairns, who once hit six sixes in 10 balls at the MCG – before the days of roped-off boundaries! So hard was he striking the ball that Australian captain Greg Chappell waved a white handkerchief in mock surrender and went to jump the long-off fence.

Using a weighty, shoulderless Newbery bat with an ultra-long handle, Cairns struck Rodney Hogg for consecutive sixes. He then lifted Dennis Lillee and Ken Macleay for two more apiece, on his way to 50 from 21 deliveries during a World Series Cup game in the early eighties. His son, Chris, was also a noted six-hitter, scoring a record 87 Test sixes.

LORD AND MASTER

Bill Watt was lord and master of the MCG wicket in the sixties and seventies. On wet days, his 'KEEP OFF' sign meant just that.

'*We* might have been putting on the show,' said Victoria's most-capped captain, Bill Lawry, 'but Bill wasn't having anyone damage *his* ground. Sometimes I'm sure he kept the outfield deliberately long, knowing some warm weather was coming. In one Shield game against Queensland, Bob Cowper and I ran two fives. That couldn't happen today, especially with the way the two long ends are roped off.'

LORD TED

Tom Veivers says England's Ted Dexter was clearly the most ferocious batsman he ever opposed. In his opening over in the MCC–Australian XI game at the MCG in 1962–63, Dexter twice dobbed Veivers into the old Southern Stand.

'I'd just watched Johnny Martin go for 39 runs from his first three overs,' said Veivers. 'Ted was a remarkable player and was really seeing them this day. He scored a century before lunch [with 13 fours and two sixes]. My first over is still imprinted on my mind. The first two I bowled, I tried to give them a tweak and they went straight through, Ted watching them go harmlessly past the off stump. The next one, he put his foot down the wicket and planted me into the grandstand. It nearly went on to the roof. He did it again the very next ball. My first over went for 14 and Johnny came past and said, "I don't feel as bad now, mate!"'

'Ted absolutely slaughtered us. All up, I went for almost 150 without taking a wicket. It knocked me right out of the game and out of contention for the Australian side for 12 months.'

SEE: MAGIC MOMENTS (I), PAGE 125

LOST OPPORTUNITIES (I)

As Bill O'Reilly was preparing to don his Australian baggy green cap for the first time (Adelaide, 1932), Australian selector Chappie Dwyer offered some words of advice.

'Keep your wits about you,' Dwyer said. 'They're already starting to say that you appeal too much for lbw.'

In O'Reilly's very first over, he struck the pads of South African Jim Christy. Wicketkeeper Bert Oldfield didn't appeal, so O'Reilly didn't either. Another two overs elapsed before umpire George Hele walked past O'Reilly and, in a quiet aside, said, 'Don't you appeal for lbw?'

'Did you think he was out, George?'

'It would have been wise, I think, for you to have asked me!'

O'Reilly said he never repeated that mistake; the Tiger was as full-throated in his appeals as anyone in the game's history.

LOST OPPORTUNITIES (II)

Alan Turner averaged less than 30 for Australia, but he did make one Test century and all but got a second, in Melbourne on New Year's Day, 1977.

'Ian Davis and I had a good morning and I got to 82 rather quickly, before becoming too confident and playing over the top of one from a little medium-pacer by the name of Asif Iqbal,' said Turner. 'I wasn't too pleased with myself and one of the selectors, Sam Loxton, was not too pleased with me either. As I walked down the stairs, he kicked me right up the bum and told me what an opportunity I'd wasted. He was right. I deserved it.'

LOVABLE LINDSAY (I)

Lindsay Hassett was one of Australia's most gifted all-round sportsmen – a superb footballer, Victorian schoolboys' tennis champion, A-grade squash player and single figure golfer. It's amazing he had time to play cricket.

From Geelong and with a huge reputation, he inexplicably struggled in his early games at South Melbourne, at one stage scoring seven ducks in a row. Off he went to the Colts, under the expert tutelage of Bert Cohen (St Kilda's famous premiership captain) and immediately prospered, scoring a big century in one of his first games.

'I was lucky, though,' said Lindsay. 'I reckon I was plumb lb first ball, but the umpire was kind. Then I was dropped twice before I scored what would have been my eighth duck on the trot, and was dropped three more times before I reached 30!'

Luck or no luck, Hassett made 142 not out and never looked back, becoming one of Australia's finest.

SEE: ONE IN A MILLION, PAGE 145

LOVABLE LINDSAY (II)

Hassett was at dinner at the Park Lane in London when a waiter accidentally tipped much of the dessert intended for the entire team down the front of his dinner suit. Calmly taking his jacket off, Hassett noticed that his trousers also needed attention. So he removed them too, and handed them to the waiter for dry-cleaning, before resuming his seat as if nothing had happened.

Hassett once told former teammate Ken Meuleman that he always had a grand time in England. 'The only time I ever got depressed,' he said, 'was on the boat, the day we were coming home.'

See: A FARTING GOOD PARTNERSHIP, page 68

LOXTON VERSUS THE WORLD

'Give me 11 Sam Loxtons,' broadcaster John Arlott once said, 'and I'll beat the world.'

One of the last players chosen on the tour of a lifetime, the Ashes tour of '48, Loxton was to play a frontline role after a back injury affected Keith Miller's capacity to bowl.

'I thought I was along for the ride,' said Loxton, 'to pull the roller if the horse broke down or something. I never thought I was going to get into that side, not with the calibre of the other players around.'

At Leeds, in the remarkable game in which Australia chased more than 400 and won, Loxton made 93 with a fistful of sixes, including several that Bill O'Reilly claimed 'landed so far back in the crowd it was almost a shilling ride in a London cab to bring them back'. On his return to the rooms, having gone for one big hit too many, Loxton was chided by Australia's cricket-loving Prime Minister, Robert Menzies, for not having made a century.

'That was a pretty stupid thing to do, Sam, so close to a century,' said Menzies.

'Haven't you made a few mistakes in your time, too, boss?' said Sam, never short of a word.

m

MADDER THAN MOST

As fast bowlers go, Rodney Hogg was madder than most. In the rooms, pre-bowling, he used to slap his own face to get nice and angry. His acid tongue and sliding bouncer became his trademark as he looked to intimidate from ball one.

'At Northcote, I'd bounce the crap out of the batsmen at practice,' Hogg said. 'No one came and told me off. In the end, I had a pretty reasonable bouncer.'

Renowned for his direct hits, his victims included world number one Viv Richards, the 'Master Blaster', in a Test match in Melbourne (1979–80). Instead of going down or showing that he had been hurt, Richards stood his ground, staring defiantly back at Hogg.

'*I* was the one in shock,' said Hogg. 'There was absolutely no reaction from Viv whatsoever. It was like a horror movie where you're filling the enemy full of bullets and yet they keep coming at you. I bounced him again next ball and he top-edged it over the fine-leg fence for six! Over my career, I reckon I bowled Viv 370 short balls and he hit 369 of them.'

Hogg's figures that day? None for 59 from six!

MAGIC MOMENTS (I)

'The Springboks had us surrounded,' said Australian all-rounder Tom Veivers, 'and we were in a spot of trouble. The wicket was starting to break up and they had two very capable left-arm bowlers in Athol McKinnon, who was a left-arm orthodox, and Trevor Goddard, who could swing the new ball and later bowl spin. Unless we changed the tempo, I couldn't see how we were going to get 'em.

'"You keep on doing what you're doing," I said to Red [Ian Redpath], "but we have to try and break them up somehow . . . I'm going to have a go."'

Set 179 runs to win the second Test and square the series after a humbling loss in the opening Test in Johannesburg, Bobby Simpson's 1966–67 Australians had lost 4/119, including Bob Cowper and Ian Chappell cheaply. While only another 60 were needed, any more quick wickets could have been disastrous.

In an earlier tour game, against Transvaal in Johannesburg, Veivers had taken to McKinnon on his way to a belligerent 94 as Australia, set almost 500, scored 413 in a fighting counterattack. The burly Queenslander resolved that if either McKinnon or Goddard pitched up, he'd try to hit with the spin towards the long-on and deep midwicket boundaries.

'I wanted to really plant one and get them thinking a bit,' said Veivers. 'If I'd missed it and was out, I would have been a bloody goose. But luckily, Goddard bowled one in the slot, I got it pretty much in the middle, and it sailed over midwicket for six. Peter van der Merwe [South Africa's captain] immediately dispensed with two of his close-catching blokes.

'It was a bit of a game of bluff. I wanted to give them the impression that I was going to have a go all the time and really take them on, like in the earlier tour match at Johannesburg.

'They went on the defensive too quickly. It enabled us to rotate the strike a bit and there was enough ones and twos around to keep it going. The next two or three overs went for 20, and we got home with less than half an hour to spare without losing another wicket.'

MAGIC MOMENTS (II)

Mick Taylor's road to first-class cricket was delayed. But, on debut for Victoria against Queensland in 1977–78, he made 75 and 107, helping the Vics to a memorable two-wicket victory after they'd been set 268 to win in the fourth innings. It was one of Taylor's signature moments in a career during which he also became one of Kim Hughes's rebel tourists to South Africa.

'Queensland was pretty confident that this was going to be the year that they finally won the Shield,' Taylor said. 'In those days, the ABC would show games [on television] from four o'clock. We got wind at lunchtime that the ABC in Queensland had arranged to bring it forward, as they thought the game would be over by teatime, with their side winning.

'But we got up and beat them. [Fast bowler] Johnny Douglas and I added 123 for the eighth wicket. I thought to myself at the time, "How long has this been going on?" It remains a very happy memory.'

MAGIC MOMENTS (III)

In all of George Tribe's 309 first-class games, never did he have a more memorable day than late in the 1946–47 season, representing Victoria against the visiting Englishmen in Melbourne. Not only did he make 60, batting at No. 9, he almost took his one and only hat-trick, *but* for inadvertently unsighting the umpire, Andy Barlow.

'We were six down overnight on the second night. We were living in Newport at the time and I caught the train up to the MCG. It stopped on the viaduct at Banana Alley and we were there for ages. I thought I would be late to the ground, so I jumped off the train, ran along the line to the street and got a taxi. "Step on it," I told the taxi driver. "I'm in next!"

'I got to the ground and a wicket fell while I was changing. I went out and went *bang, bang, bang*, made 60, and then got six-for [6/49 from 14.5 overs]. I had two wickets in two balls, and Alec Bedser came in and knocked the cover off his first ball [through to the wicketkeeper]. Up I went, only for Andy Barlow to give it not out. I asked him what had happened and he said, "You ran in front of me, George. I couldn't see!"

'Alec was walking, too . . . and I never did take a first-class hat-trick.'

SEE: THE BALL OF HIS LIFE, PAGE 15

MAN OVERBOARD

Most thought it a good laugh when a man was deliberately tipped out of a boat and into the Hawkesbury River at Berowra one Sunday afternoon – until the man's wife yelled, 'Grab him! He can't swim!'

His companion duly dived in and pulled him to safety. The rescued man? A young Don Bradman.

MASSIE'S MATCH

It was the ultimate sporting fairytale – 16 wickets in his debut Test *and* at Lord's, the historic home of cricket. For Bob Massie, a quietly spoken kid from the west with a rare gift for prodigious swing and John Arlott impersonations, it was the signature three-and-a-half days of his career, and remains one of the great moments in Ashes folklore. Then 25, Massie was at the height of his powers and grateful for the opportunity to tour England with a group he describes as lifelong mates and true champions, both on and off the field.

The assembled squad was from all over mainland Australia and had vastly different backgrounds, from knockabouts like Rod Marsh and Dennis Lillee, to the highly educated and very cultured Paul Sheahan.

Within days of their arrival in the Old Country, Massie said there was a camaraderie that made this team-on-the-rise highly potent and united. There were midnight singsongs and a riotous recording session of 'Here Come the Aussies' – which somehow made it into the Top 10 hits on the charts in Sydney! The team, under a master captain in Ian Chappell, was one of the happiest.

Massie had played in Scotland for three years and was off to a flier at Worcester, taking six wickets in an innings and sending down seven maidens in a row. But for injury, he would have been in the side for the first Test of the tour. He was taking a bit of stick at Ilford in the final lead-up match to Lord's, before Chappell put his mind at rest. 'You're in. Just relax.'

The morning of his debut was one of those typically overcast London mornings where you could almost reach up and touch the grey clouds. With Lillee bounding in downhill from the Pavilion end, and Massie's swing exaggerated by his tactic of going round the wicket to the left-handers, the Australians made immediate inroads. Brian Luckhurst lost his off stump to a high-pace Lillee special, before Massie burst through Geoff Boycott's defences with a full-length swinger. What a first-up Test wicket – the famed Yorkshireman, renowned as virtually unbowlable, out for just a dozen!

It was a story-line straight from *Boy's Own Annual* and, with two bags of eight-for, debutant Massie dominated like no one before him, bar Jim Laker.

'MASTER, EVER THOUGHT ABOUT RETIRING?'

One of the earlier books I helped co-write was Terry Jenner's *T. J. Over the Top*, a warts-and-all life story of the only Australian Test cricketer to do time. T. J.'s work with Shane Warne – they first met when Terry was on parole – is a major part of the book, and he remains a mentor to Warne 15 years on.

Knowing that I was also a leg-spinner, albeit of club standard, T. J. would offer a tip or two, hoping I could get a bagful and earn promotion from the Frankston Peninsula thirds. It never happened and, late in my 10-year tenure there as third XI captain, I sent T. J. an SOS email. I explained that my leg-spinner wasn't spinning and that I was struggling to dismiss even the club's practice captain, who was in his late fifties and hadn't batted in a game for years.

A return email soon lobbed and I opened it with great relish, thinking that here could be the elixir of life. Maybe I wasn't powering through the crease. Maybe my bowling arm wasn't trailing across as it should . . .

'Master,' wrote T. J., 'ever thought about retiring?'

THE MILLER–BRADMAN FEUD

It was Don Bradman's last appearance at the Sydney Cricket Ground. As the champion was marking guard in the Kippax-Oldfield testimonial game, a virtual Test trial for the upcoming tour of South Africa, Keith Miller walked past Sam Loxton at mid-off and said, 'I'm going to give the little bugger one . . . I don't think he likes 'em.'

In his penultimate appearance in first-class cricket, 40-year-old Bradman hadn't batted for more than 10 weeks. Rather than bowl a welcoming one well-up on the leg stump so the Don could flick it to square-leg for a starting single (a favourite practice), Miller sent one searing past Bradman's cap.

'It was a monster,' said Loxton. 'Certainly not the one to get off the mark. It went straight past [Bradman's] nose. Nugget walked back past me and said, "He didn't like that one. I'm going to give him another."'

This time, Bradman, with all his competitive juices flowing, struck it just forward of square, like a rocket, straight into the fence.

'If the fence and stand hadn't been there,' Loxton said, 'it would have gone all the way to George Street in the CBD. He absolutely creamed it. Miller walked past me again and said, "Okay, I take it all back!"'

Miller's omission from the touring team, several weeks later, remains one of the foremost selection sensations and, while he conveniently blamed mediocre form, he had made more than 400 first-class runs and taken 11 wickets that season, and was the glamorous face of the Australian game. While he was later to reinforce the 1949–50 side, after Bill Johnston was injured in a car accident, his omission rankled and was central to the long-time antipathy between him and Bradman. Miller believed Bradman to be jealous of his popularity and even in his final, wheelchair-bound years, threatened to go public with his views. Only his friendship with Bradman's son, John, stopped him.

SEE: THE QUICKEST SINCE '38, PAGE 167

MIMICKING THE LEGENDS

The sheer fun of cricket invariably bubbles close to the surface. Ask Ian Healy, who loved to do Merv Hughes impersonations, complete with exaggerated follow-through, at practice or in charity matches. England's Ken Barrington could mimic the many mannerisms of Australian all-rounder Ken Mackay, including his muscle-bound walk, dangling bat and vigorous gum-chewing action.

NSW's Warren Saunders was also a great card and, late

in one Prime Minister's XI match (1959), mimicked the actions of all the main bowlers – including the England expressmen Freddie Trueman and Peter Loader, as well as Keith Miller's famous toss of his hair before bowling. He had the Englishmen roaring with laughter when he took his run-up almost back to the boundary and steamed in like Frank 'Typhoon' Tyson.

'Could only do it for one ball, though,' he quipped. 'It's too far to run!' Saunders reckoned Typhoon ran in so far that 'you were out of form by the time he got to the stumps'.

MORRIE SPOILS THE PARTY

Victorian fast bowler Ernie McCormick had taken all nine South Australian wickets (Adelaide, 1936–37). As South Australian tailender Graham Williams was checking his guard, Victorian captain Hans Ebeling was telling Morrie 'Molly' Sievers, who was coming on at the other end, to bowl as wide as possible to give McCormick a chance at all 10.

'The first two were so wide I almost took 'em at second slip,' said McCormick. 'Harry on the trams knew what was going on. Hans was fielding at [first] slip and motioned to Molly to get 'em over a bit, and he landed his next on middle stump, clean bowling Williams. And that was that.'

McCormick finished with nine for 40 and 12 wickets for the match.

THE MOST COLOURFUL TOURING TEAM

With names like Punch, Ping-Pong, Friday, King Billy and Flibbertigibbet, they just had to be the most colourful touring team of all. The 1907–08 Fijians may have been a little short on cricketing ability, but they were highly

Ever-so-modest, ever-so-humble Bill Ponsford (right) with his long-time Victorian opening partner, Bill Woodfull.

INSET: Ponny aged 79 and still showing the full face of the bat.
JOHN HART/CRICKETER MAGAZINE

Cartoonist-cricketer Arthur Mailey loved to draw 'Patsy' Hendren, the evergreen and universally popular Englishman who toured down-under three times.

MAILEY/CRICKET SKETCHES

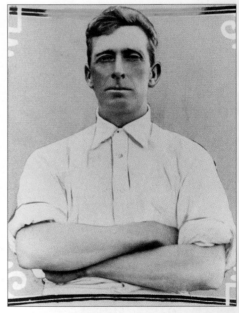

Not great with names, Don Blackie called almost everyone 'Rock'.

The 1930 Aussies were the first Ashes party to include a young Don Bradman, (the Don is sitting second from the right, next to captain Bill Woodfull). Victor Richardson, the Chappells' grandfather, is sitting second from the left.

Funnyman Ernie McCormick (far right) cuts a strapping figure at the Victoria Falls Hotel swimming pool during a day off for the 1935–36 touring Australians.

Time for a smoke: Australian captain Vic Richardson (centre) and guide at the top of Table Mountain, 1935.

Ernie McCormick (left) and Bill Brown on board ship on the way back from South Africa, March 1936.

Vic Richardson (pointing) with fellow Australians and a group
of Zulu women at Karridene in South Africa, 1936.

Leo O'Brien overheard the famous Woodfull/Plum
Warner conversation in Adelaide in 1933.

Harry 'Bull' Alexander tending his Euroa garden in later life. Australia's captain, Bill Woodfull, stopped him from bowling Bodyline in the 1932–33 Test against England in Sydney.

DOES HALCOMBE THROW?

The Victorian umpire considered that he did, and no-balled him six times.

Just to prove what does actually happen, when this young Western Australian hurls the leather at the wicket a slow-motion film was taken, and you may see for yourself, at

THE REGENT

of course.

The film will be shown at all sessions.

A childhood accident forced Ron Halcombe to develop a peculiar wristy action. He was sensationally no-balled for throwing in a Sheffield Shield match in Melbourne. Cine-film of his action was made and shown at theatres such as Melbourne's Regent.

Tom Hutchison

Bill 'Tiger' O'Reilly was a powerhouse both on and off the field, and friend and mentor to dozens of Australia's cricket journalists.

enthusiastic and very popular, too, with their novel costumes and pre-match chants. In Melbourne, 9000 people paid a total of £225 to see them on the opening day of their game against a Victorian XI.

The team captain was Prince Ratu Kadavu Levi, the hereditary Prince of Fiji. An excellent batsman, he'd wear pads but no gloves and, in the field, chase down even the hardest-hit balls. At Newcastle, he also rescued two men from drowning!

His nephew, Ratu Pope, made 127 in less than two hours in a game against Southern Tasmania in Hobart. As a token of appreciation for the wonderful entertainment he had provided, he was presented with a gold badge in the shape of Tasmania.

The Fijians played at outposts from West Maitland through to Wangaratta. The only downside, they said, was the grass seeds, which tended to stick into their bare feet.

MOTZ MAYHEM

It was some of the most savage hitting ever seen at the Adelaide Oval. New Zealander Dick Motz made 82 in an hour in a tour match against South Australia in 1967–68. Ten of his fours, and many of his sixes, came against a young Ian Chappell, who had three overs of leg spin smashed for 62.

'Dick had big shoulders and a big upper body, and he hit Chappelli all over the ballpark,' said Chappell's teammate and prominent radio personality-to-be, Ken Cunningham. He almost hit one ball into St Peter's Cathedral. They were some of the biggest hits I've ever seen.

'Finally I caught him, off Ian, on the straight hit [of 103.5 metres], just a metre in from the fence at the River Torrens end, right on the old kick-off line for the footballers.'

Cunningham says the only comparable hit at the

Adelaide Oval in his time was one towering six by England's Ted Dexter against Garry Sobers. It was off the second new ball during an MCC tour match in 1962–63, and it steepled high over the members' grandstand and on to the tennis courts. 'You don't tend to forget shots like that,' he said. 'It was huge.'

MR CRICKET OF WESTERN AUSTRALIA

No one was prouder, or more responsible, than Barry Shepherd when seven home-grown West Australians were chosen in the Australian team for the Perth Test of 1981–82.

Had he been born on the eastern seaboard rather than in the less influential west, Shepherd's record as one of Australia's foremost postwar left-handers would have been even more impressive. He was to play just 11 Tests, with an average of 40-plus. His international opportunities were limited by the considerable top-order competition from Norm O'Neill, Bob Cowper, Brian Booth and Peter Burge, and the apathy of selectors who for years scorned the skills of cricketers from across the Nullarbor Plain.

Hugely influential in West Australian cricket's renaissance on and off the ground in the sixties, Shepherd's way of bridging the cricketing Iron Curtain was to work his players like footballers. For fielding-only nights, he got them to turn up in old clothes and insisted they slide around, saving runs. Not only did the team's fielding skills improve, the new professionalism saw WA win in Sydney for the first time in history, in 1965–66. (Shepherd himself was primarily responsible, with a defiant 88 not out.) Within two years, the previously unfashionable westerners won the Sheffield Shield for the first time under a full roster of games.

Captain for five years, Shepherd promoted youngsters, often before their time.

'No one was more parochial towards WA cricket or possessed more cricketing foresight than Shep,' said ex-teammate and Testman, Terry Jenner. 'He saw the big picture and felt we could win the respect of the eastern states, and nurture more Test cricketers, by working harder and encouraging risk-takers.'

MR PACKER, I PRESUME?

In his comeback to international cricket, Ian Redpath scored a century against a Rest of the World attack including Imran Khan and Mike Procter at VFL Park, Waverley.

'I wasn't so used to making runs and I was still stiff two days later,' Redpath said of his World Series return.

Later that week, on a freezing day in his home town of Geelong, he asked for a bowl. Clive Lloyd was caught in the covers from one Redpath claimed to have 'held back a little'. In jubilation, Redpath jumped and turned in midair, snapping his Achilles! During his hospitalisation in Geelong, among many visitors and well-wishers was the big boss himself, Kerry Packer.

'It was a very nice gesture,' said Redders. 'He was a very generous man and organised for me to have a telly because there was none in the room. He'd come down by helicopter. He didn't have to do it, but I was very appreciative.'

Redpath said World Series Cricket was hard work. 'We were all over the place but in the end, as I said to my wife, we couldn't afford not to do it.'

MUTHIAH MURALIDARAN'S
TEN BEST BOWLERS

Two Australians, Shane Warne and Glenn McGrath, were rated among the top 10 bowlers of Muthiah Muralidaran's first 10 years in world cricket.

The little spin-wizard ranked Pakistan's Wasim Akram, with his ability to 'bowl anything from outswingers to slow', as the greatest bowler of the modern era. 'He truly mastered his art,' Murali said. Warne was placed second and McGrath fifth; only their modest returns on subcontinental wickets cost them higher slots.

'I love to watch the way Shane bowls,' Murali said. 'He's so confident and puts the batsman under so much pressure. His character is good for the game. Until 2004 and the Indian tour, he didn't have much success in the subcontinent, as the wickets are very slow and he is used to the extra bounce of Australian wickets. He needs the bounce to be at his absolute best. But he bowled very well, especially on that tour.'

MURALI'S TOP TEN BOWLERS
1. Wasim Akram (Pakistan)
2. Shane Warne (Australia)
3. Courtney Walsh (West Indies)
4. Curtly Ambrose (West Indies)
5. Glenn McGrath (Australia)
6. Waqar Younis (Pakistan)
7. Darren Gough (England)
8. Anil Kumble (India)
9. Saqlain Mushtaq (Pakistan)
10. Daniel Vettori (New Zealand)

n
||||||||||||

NEIL HARVEY'S FINEST HOUR

Of all his 21 Test centuries, Neil Harvey says one stands out, even ahead of his fabled century on debut against England in 1948.

'It was the ton I made on an uncovered wicket at Durban in South Africa in '49–'50,' he says. 'Durban's climate is very similar to Brisbane and there were some big thunderstorms during that match. After South Africa had made 300-odd, we were caught on a real sticky and bowled out for 75. Hughie Tayfield, their great off-spinner, took seven for 23.

'Dudley Nourse, their captain, thought he'd get a weather forecast from the bureau. They told him another storm was coming and instead of following us on, he decided to bat, thinking it would be better if we batted last. Storms were all around us. It seemed to be raining everywhere but at the actual ground, and the Springboks batted and kept on batting.

'We had a very clever captain in Lindsay Hassett – probably the best captain I played under. He told all the bowlers – Ray Lindwall, Keith Miller, Billy Johnston and Ian Johnson – to bowl as straight as they could. "Don't do anything with the ball. We'll try and keep 'em in!" he said.

'The boys kept them in as long as they could, but we still got them out for less than 100, leaving us 336 to win. The wicket wasn't brilliant and there were lots of marks. In addition to Tayfield, they had Tufty Mann, who was also a good spinner.

'It was one of my more uncharacteristic innings, a long one. I ended up getting 151 not out. Sam [Loxton] and I had a big partnership [of 145], and Colin McCool and I were there at the end [having added 106]. I was thinking of giving it away when we got close to their total. Col came down and convinced me to keep going and be there at the finish.

'Had Nourse followed us on, there's no doubt we would have lost the game. As it was, we were 3/59 and then 4/95, batting on a day-four wicket. It was a great thrill to get up.'

THE NET SESSION FROM HELL

At just 165 cm (5'6"), standing on his tippy toes, Greg Shipperd (now coach of the Victorian Bush-rangers) was more easily able to evade bouncers than taller players. He just wishes helmets were invented earlier.

'We were in the nets in Sydney one day and Garth Le Roux [the South African expressman] happened to be there, bowling side-by-side [with] Dennis Lillee . . . They were trying to outdo each other and I was the meat in the sandwich. It was as if they were having a bowl-off to see who was faster and, for 20 minutes, I faced the fastest and most aggressive bowling, apart from Thommo, I ever faced throughout my entire career.

'It was particularly challenging in those days, without helmets. You had to fend for yourself. It was pretty bruising stuff. Thankfully, they did develop helmets, and it was less physically hurtful to spend a net session against guys like Dennis. Not that he'd ever let up on you. He brought the same competitiveness into club cricket, too. He was flat out in any game he played.

'As a teenager, in my very first trial game, I'm sure he thought this little bloke shouldn't be here. He really gave me a working over, and did in subsequent games as well. I thought this is what the top level must be like. Mentally, I was prepared for the future.

'Dennis was a master craftsman at what he did. His game plans were simply outstanding. He'd work a batsman over mentally and physically. He did it so well and so consistently. I was in awe of his competitiveness, power and ability.

'He was also such a great team man; a great giver of knowledge and encouragement to his teammates. When he walked into a room, the place would light up. It still does. I'm proud to call him one of my mates.'

NEVER ANY DOUBT

Terry Alderman was a notable No. 11 – and third in line in a Wasim Akram hat-trick one year in Sharjah. Returning to the Australian dressing-room, he said, 'There was never any doubt, was there!'

NEVER UPSET A FAST BOWLER

The summer he was selected for his one and only Test match (1951–52), Victorian opener George Thoms was playing for the first time against Ray Lindwall and New South Wales at the MCG. During an interlude, he told Lindwall that he was nothing like as fast as he'd remembered him as a hero-worshipping schoolboy.

'I was leaning on my bat, waiting for Neil Harvey to come in at the fall of a wicket,' said Thoms. 'As soon as I said it, I realised what a stupid thing it was to have said, but we were going along nicely at 1/90 or so. Ray walked past [teammate] Sid Barnes and said, "I'll show that little bastard just how fast I can bowl."

'He never did forgive me. Every time I played against him after that, the first thing he would do was to come up, look me straight in the eye and say, "Any more statements before I bowl?"

'They are a different breed, fast bowlers. I learnt a lesson that day: never upset a fast bowler.'

NEW YEAR'S CELEBRATION

For all of Alan Davidson's monumental achievements in cricket, including 44 Tests, he'll never forget the opening half-hour of the second Test in Melbourne on New Year's Eve, 1959, as England crashed to 1/7, 2/7 and then 3/7 in one over.

'It was a warmish morning in Melbourne,' Davidson said. 'There was just a touch of moisture in the top of the wicket and the ball was moving.

'The great gift that I was born with was that I could actually move a ball. The first one, poor old Richo [Peter Richardson], could always find the edge for me. There were a lot of players who weren't good enough to find the edge, but he was good enough. Willie Watson [No. 3] I got with a yorker and Tom Graveney [No. 4] got the unplayable one [veering back late and capturing him lbw] . . . That was one of the best balls I honestly believe I ever bowled . . . My elation on that particular day [was enormous] . . . You never dream of getting three-for in an over.'

Seven weeks later, in a Sheffield Shield match in Adelaide, 'Davo' took three wickets in four balls – new-ball striking at its best!

NEW ZEALAND SWANSONG

So sore and immobilised was legendary Bill O'Reilly after the Wellington Test of 1945–46 that he threw his

AUSTRALIAN TESTMEN TO TAKE THREE OR MORE WICKETS IN AN OVER*

FOUR WICKETS
Jason Gillespie, v. England, Perth, 1998–99

THREE WICKETS
Alan Davidson v. England, Melbourne, 1958–59
Johnny Martin, v. West Indies, Melbourne, 1960–61
Glenn McGrath, v. West Indies, Perth, 2000–01
Carl Rackemann, v. Pakistan, Adelaide, 1989–90
Shane Warne, v. England, Brisbane, 1994–95
Shane Warne, v. England, Melbourne, 1994–95

* Tests on home soil since 1955

bowling boots out the window. 'Won't be needing these again,' he told teammates.

NINE HOURS TO CROSS THE TASMAN

Flying was a rarity for touring teams until the sixties. However, the 1945–46 team to New Zealand did cross the Tasman by air in a tiny seaplane, the *Catalina*, whose top speed was 140 mph.

'We took off from Rushcutters Bay, having been ferried out to the plane in a small boat,' said one of the chosen Australians, Ken Meuleman. 'I don't know how 13 of us, plus baggage and manager [Son Yeomans] all fitted in. Most of us stood all the way. Lindsay Hassett commandeered the bunk and was the only one to get any sleep. All up, it took us nine hours to get there – and the actual Test match only went for eight!'

'NO ONE CHARGES THE GREAT D. K.'

An inspiration to a whole generation of fast bowlers, Dennis Lillee continued his headliner ways in the early eighties and beyond, even playing a season of English county cricket with Northamptonshire into his fortieth year.

Aged 45, his Melbourne farewell was for Dean Jones's testimonial. He ran in as usual from his favourite southern end and saw his first ball unceremoniously whacked over point by the then-teenage Victorian, Brad Hodge. The next one was about three yards quicker and flicked a retreating Hodge's armpit on its way through to Lillee's old mate Rodney Marsh, who burst out laughing.

'No one charges the great D. K.,' said Marsh.

NO VICS

Victorians were among every Australian team until the Adelaide Test of 1976–77 (Test No. 360), when the only Victorian named was the Tasmanian-born Max Walker, as twelfth man. Gary Cosier, selected at No. 6, was then representing South Australia.

0

|||||||||||||

AN OLD FAVOURITE

When David Hookes was selected for the Centenary Test, he insisted on using a favourite old bat, complete with vellum reinforcing. His sponsor, Gray-Nicolls, had offered him any number of new blades, but Hookes wanted something tried and true. He duly made 17 and 56 on debut, including his much-celebrated five fours in a row against England's captain, Tony Greig.

'It wasn't even a Gray-Nicolls. It was a Stuart Surridge Jumbo,' said Hookes, years later. 'I'd been across to Dulwich in 1975 and one of our players, Peter Rice, worked with Stuart. Their new bat was the Jumbo and he gave me one. There wasn't a lot of SS gear around; certainly not a lot of good bats to choose from, anyway. But this was a favourite bat so, when I got back to Australia, I put Gray-Nicolls stickers on it, used it during that [1976–77] season, and again in the Ashes series in '77, before it finally fell over.'

Hookes gave the bat to a private collector before borrowing it back for a re-enactment of that Centenary Test innings for a 25-years-on television special.

'It was in an untouched state . . . still with all the old tape around it, too. A familiar old friend,' he said.

OLD-TIME SPORTSMANSHIP

It was Sam Loxton's first time in a Victorian XII, and he was responsible for bringing the drinks on to the field. As

143

three o'clock approached, he arranged the cordials and was about to step on to the MCG, pleased as punch in his dark-blue Victorian blazer, only to be stopped at the gate by a call from Victoria's captain, Lindsay Hassett.

'I was counting the balls and as soon as the umpire called "Over", I was on – only for Lindsay to tell me to stop, and point towards the scoreboard,' Loxton said. 'Denis Compton was on 99 and duly got his century during that [following] over. "Lad, you never bring the drinks on the ground when a bloke is on 99," Lindsay told me, in no uncertain terms.'

It was a lesson in etiquette that Loxton never forgot.

OLLIE'S 'GABBA SPREE

When Colin 'Ollie' Milburn was originally left out of England's winter tour to Pakistan (1968), he came to Western Australia as a man on a mission. Once dubbed 'as tidy as an unmade bed', the heavyweight right-hander took his frustrations out on platoons of Australian bowlers in almost every mainland city. His series of explosive innings included a double-century against Queensland that remains one of the most famous ever at the 'Gabba. His 243 in just four hours included an Australian-record 181 from 134 balls between lunch and tea. In all, he hit 38 fours and four sixes.

'It was the most extraordinary two hours' batting I have ever seen,' West Australia's senior batsman John Inverarity told writer Mark Browning. 'Milburn played shot after shot – drives, cuts and pulls, almost at will. But they were all strokes. There was no suggestion that he was slogging. He hit two and three balls an over, every over, to the boundary.'

Milburn and Derek Chadwick added 328 for the first wicket, against a competitive attack that included three Test bowlers – Peter Allan, Ross Duncan and the Indian international, Rusi Surti.

With 940 Sheffield Shield runs at an average of 60-plus, Milburn was to earn a late recall into the English team, and made 139 in the third Test at Karachi. Sadly, it was to be his last Test innings. Just six weeks later, he lost the sight of one eye after a car accident in England.

ONE IN A MILLION

Diminutive, dapper, devilish Lindsay Hassett played into his fifties, including one memorable appearance for Prime Minister Robert Menzies' XI against Peter May's touring Englishmen at Canberra's Manuka Oval (1958–59). His close mate from Test days, Arthur Morris, led off with 79 and, when it was Lindsay's turn to bat, he asked Morris if he could borrow his bat. He was soon back in the pavilion, but not before handing the borrowed blade – one of Morris's favourites – to a small boy in the crowd.

'What a wonderful gesture that was from Lindsay,' said an admiring Menzies.

'What do you mean, sir?' asked Morris, who hadn't seen the presentation.

'Lindsay just gave his bat away as he was coming back into the pavilion.'

When the lucky recipient knocked on the pavilion door and asked if the players could sign it for him, Hassett grinned. He acted as MC and made all the introductions. 'And Mr Morris, in particular, would love to sign it, son,' he said.

ONE OF THE ALL-TIME GREAT SPELLS

So sore was Keith Miller's knee just 24 hours before the 1954–55 Melbourne Test that he felt he had little option but to withdraw. But at the prompting of his close mate, champion jockey Scobie Breasley, Miller went and saw a horse veterinarian mate of Breasley's. The treatment was so successful that, against the odds, he took his place in the field the next morning.

'And he bowled sharp, too,' said wicketkeeper Len Maddocks, playing his first Test. 'Whatever the bloke did to his knee worked. By lunchtime, Keith had three for 5. The wicket had a green tinge in it, but it was still one of the all-time great spells.'

ONE-TEST WONDER

Matthew Nicholson was sitting on a plane at Perth Airport, ready to return home to his family in Sydney for the Christmas break, when he was informed that he should return to the terminal; he had a cricket match to play. Then 24, Nicholson thought he must have forgotten to factor in a one-day game for Western Australia.

'I borrowed a mobile phone from the bloke next door and rang Jane Parsons at the WACA. She confirmed I'd been included in Australia's Ashes Test team – and for the Christmas Test, the biggest match on the calendar,' he said. 'Jason Gillespie had dropped out [injured] and I was to be his replacement. At that stage, I'd played only eight or nine first-class games, and had really only got back to cricket at the start of that season after the previous 18 months out [with chronic fatigue syndrome].

'I wasn't too nervous, as I was in pretty good form at the time. I was full of the joy of getting back to play cricket again and that's probably why I played so well, as I didn't care about anything else. I'd had my ups and downs, but being carefree and going out to play was what it was all about.'

Nicholson took one for 59 and three for 56 on debut. It remains his one and only Test match.

OPPORTUNITY KNOCKS (I)

When, leading into the 1992 tour of Sri Lanka, Australian captain Allan Border saw Shane Warne at Melbourne's Tullamarine Airport, he did a double take.

'You could see he wanted to be a Test player,' Border said. 'He'd shed a lot of weight, had a haircut, and his attitude was absolutely outstanding. There was no question he had special talents. But he then had to go away and do a bit of work, which he did. Credit to him.'

One of the key factors in Warne's new hunger for cricket and desire to make the most of his opportunity had been a heart-to-heart chat in Adelaide with his coach, Terry Jenner. Warne had arrived with some drinks that he wanted to share with Jenner and Cricket Academy head coach Rod Marsh, as a thank you for their efforts during the previous six months.

Jenner had been itching for the chance to tell Warne that to truly succeed, hard work was only the beginning. Warne could easily disappear as quickly as he'd arrived, Jenner told him, and regret the wasted opportunity for the rest of his life. He asked Warne how many sacrifices he'd made to make the Australian XI. Warne couldn't think of even one. He liked a drink, and he smoked and partied like any 21-year-old.

Just over a month later, Warne's mother, Brigitte, rang Jenner and said, 'I don't know what you said to Shane, Terry, but it's working. He's been running six days a week and on the seventh day he plays golf.'

Warne lost more than 10 kilograms that winter. In the opening Test in Sri Lanka, he took three for 11 on the last afternoon, to lead an incredible Australian win and launch one of the truly great Test careers.

OPPORTUNITY KNOCKS (II)

Not only was Sid Barnes a champion batsman, he was a showman, a firebrand and an opportunist who saw his selection for the 1948 tour of war-ravaged England as a chance to make some cash on the side, wheeling and dealing. Arthur Morris became so tired of goods being bought and sold from the hotel room he was sharing with Barnes that he requested a transfer!

Barnes also had a heart of gold. When a young Alan Davidson was chosen for his first tour of England in 1953, Barnes gave him his cricket bag, saying, 'Son, I won't be needing this any more.'

OPPOSING HIS HEROES

As a 15-year-old, Wayne Clark made his first XI debut for Bassendean-Bayswater (now Bayswater-Morley) in an A-grade semifinal in Perth. Among the opposition from Nedlands was Bob Cowper, one of only three Australians to score a triple-century in an Ashes Test match. Clark was tall and skinny and had been playing fourth-grade all year. Cowper thrashed all the bowlers, Clark included.

The following season, Clark opposed his hero, Graham 'Garth' McKenzie – one of West Australian cricket's golden greats, who deliberately bowled nothing but half-volleys. For WA kids like Clark and other Test players-to-be, playing against the best on a Saturday afternoon on flat, bouncy wickets was part of one's apprenticeship and never to be forgotten. Clark says it was an ideal prelude to representative challenges, and he looks back on his formative days with the greatest of affection.

ORBIT-BOUND

The best single shot Gippsland cricket legend Trevor Steer ever saw was by a batsman from the Morwell River Prison Farm who, one day in the early eighties, hit him straight over extra cover for six.

'Every now and again, someone would turn up who could really play,' Steer said. 'This shot not only went for six, it finished about three paddocks across. It was extraordinary. I never did find out who it was (you didn't always get their right names). But he played good cricket!'

OUT OF THIS WORLD

One of Australia's secrets to success in the seventies and early eighties was its fielding flair, especially among its slipsmen. The Chappell brothers and Allan Border were all magnificent close-in catchers. Fast bowler Rodney Hogg says one catch taken by Greg Chappell at the start of Melbourne's Ashes thriller in 1982–83 was simply 'out of this world'.

'It was going down the leg side to [Graeme] Foxy Fowler, a left-hander, and everyone – including Rod [Marsh] – was following it, when it hit the outside edge. Greg was unsighted by Fowler's body and didn't get any sort of view of it until the last possible instant. He caught it like he was plucking peaches in his backyard. It was a remarkable catch and a real bonus for me.'

SEE: SECRETS OF SUCCESS, PAGE 178

OUTLAWED

The day long-striding Test prospect Ron Halcombe was no-balled for throwing remains among the most

sensational cricketing days ever in Melbourne. A product
of St Peter's College in Adelaide, Halcombe had played
A-grade cricket at 18 and state cricket at 20, despite
having only three full fingers on his right hand since
childhood.

Having broken the nose of Englishman George
Geary in the opening tour match of 1928–29, Halcombe
joined Victoria's 'Bull' Alexander and South Australia's
Tim Wall among the most likely pace prospects for the
1930 tour of England. He regarded the game against the
Victorians in mid-January 1930 as the most important of
his career, after switching to Western Australia.

It was a working day in Melbourne and few more than
2000 were in for the start. WA were out in just four and a
half hours and, with just over an hour to play, Halcombe,
then 23, was ready to blitz the Vics. His first two or three
balls to Victorian opener Leo O'Brien were just warm-ups,
but displayed his peculiar, exaggerated wrist action. He
quickened his step on the fourth and let go a flier, only for
square-leg umpire Andy Barlow to call, 'No-ball'.

Halcombe stopped mid-pitch, thunderstruck. His
captain, Dick Bryant, ran to Barlow for an explanation.
The umpire flexed his elbow and indicated that Halcombe
had thrown the ball.

Halcombe was to be no-balled six times in a row, with
two of the calls coming late, after the ball was already
nestling in wicketkeeper Bob Hewson's gloves. At the
sixth call, a dazed Halcombe threw the ball to Bryant
and trudged away from the crease, before being cajoled
to return and finish the over, off only a few steps. His
13-ball over had taken 10 minutes to complete and he
was not to bowl again in the match.

A week later, in Hobart, he was no-balled 10 times
in a row for throwing, and 12 times for the match. His
English tour aspirations were dead and buried.

'I had to rely on my wrist for a lot of my pace because

my large finger was just a stump,' Halcombe said. 'From the age of two onwards, I had to hold the ball differently to others. I had only one finger to bowl with, so every day as I walked the two miles to school and back, I would squeeze a stone and exercise my wrist to a point where it had incredible elasticity.

'After Barlow called me, I approached him at lunch and asked where I was throwing from. He told me the wrist. I suppose it's a question of whether you're fast or slow.'

The *Australasian* reported that 'Halcombe was broken-hearted and showed natural distress in the dressing-rooms after the match, and regarded it as the finish of his cricket career. It was a cruel blow for Halcombe as he practically lived for his bowling and, in his heart, felt that he still had a chance of getting into the Australian XI.'

While Halcombe was to remain in the game, and once took four wickets in four balls in Perth grade cricket (1936), he was never again in Test contention. In one of his last first-class matches, against Keith Rigg's visiting Victorians in 1939, he took five for 40, including the Victorian top four: Rigg, Ian Lee, Lindsay Hassett and Gordon Tamblyn.

At the height of Halcombe's no-ball controversy, Hoyts made a slow-motion film of his action and played it as part of their regular sessions at theatres such as Melbourne's Regent. Halcombe received dozens of sympathy letters, including one from 'two little girls' who said they hoped umpire Barlow would develop appendicitis and not be able to umpire again so they could see Halcombe bowl! It took pride of place in his scrapbook.

OUTSCORING THE DON

Having already carried his bat earlier in the tour at Lord's, in-form Australian opener Bill Brown seemed set to do it again, only to be the last man out at The Oval in 1938.

'It was the only thing I was disappointed about,' Brown said. 'I'd batted right through, only to fall to a catch at fine leg slip for 60-odd [69]. And I got out to someone who rarely ever bowled, in their left-hand batsman, Maurice Leyland.'

That was the game in which England started with a record 7/903 declared, the Australians being forced to bat two men short after Don Bradman and Jack Fingleton were injured. With 512 runs in the series of his life, Brown made more runs than anyone on either side, Bradman included.

OVER AND TIME

Representing the Lords Taverners in a celebrity charity match at Windsor Castle one day, ex-Testman Terry Jenner found himself bowling to romance actor Robert Powell and another very English gent sporting an MCC egg-and-bacon cap.

Come the last over of the day, much to his frustration, Jenner hadn't taken a wicket (no one was too bothered about chasing any high catches). He reckoned he'd taken wickets in almost all the important cricket-playing countries, and wanted to get at least one in England.

After Powell had taken a single from a skyer to mid-wicket that fell safely between four fielders, Jenner turned to Powell and said, 'Right, your mate's going to cop the whole repertoire, now!'

'I came in and bowled as quick and as hard-spun a leg-break as I could, and he missed it by a foot. The follow-up was the hardest, quickest-spun wrong 'un I could bowl and, as he went across to cover it, it darted back and hit him in his chest! I completed the over with a series of deliveries, all of which either beat his bat or hit him in the body.

'Last ball of the over, I bowled my trademark ball, the

slider. He flashed at it, nicked it, and David Cowper, our 'keeper, took the catch. "Howzzzat, umpire?" I said.

'The umpire, an Englishman, looked at me and said, "No, not out. And I hope you feel proud of yourself, son. The guy you were bowling to is 73 years old. Over. And Time."'

OVERRULED

Only once in the last 90 years have the wishes of an Australian selection panel been overruled. In 1951–52, Don Bradman, Jack Ryder and Chappie Dwyer included the brash opener Sid Barnes in their proposed XII, only for the Board of Control to send back the team and ask that they reconvene. Barnes, who hadn't played a Test since 1948, was not considered a suitable choice – as it proved, for reasons other than cricket. (The provocative Barnes had a habit of upsetting officialdom. After retiring prematurely – because, he claimed, cricket didn't pay him enough – he took a series of swipes at officials in his hardhitting Sydney newspaper column.)

Before 1912, when six of Australia's leading players boycotted the triangular Test tour, the players themselves had been solely responsible for selection. In the earliest days, they had also split the gate receipts directly with their international visitors, a custom that disappeared after Board intervention.

OXLADE'S BIG MOMENT

When Ballarat left-hander Peter Oxlade made 95 in the game of his life against New Zealand in the New Year of '81, his name was on the front page of virtually every newspaper around the country. Not because of his knock, mind you, but because *he* was knocked – almost unconscious – by New Zealand's champion strike bowler, Richard Hadlee.

When a young kid dared to call Hadlee an 'animal' as he was walking off Geelong's Kardinia Park soon afterwards, Hadlee chased and admonished the boy, creating an international incident, and ill will for the rest of the tour.

'It wasn't Richard's fault, it was mine,' said Oxlade, years later. 'Helmets were just starting to appear back then and one of the New Zealanders, John Parker, wandered up to me when a wicket fell in the first over and said, "This bloke [Hadlee] is pretty fiery. And he's quick, too. Haven't thought about getting a helmet, have you?"

'I told him it was the biggest game of cricket in my life. I didn't want to change now and put on a bit of new equipment which I wasn't used to. It was a decision which was to haunt me!'

The crowd had swelled to almost 1000, thanks to the scheduling of a twilight session, and Oxlade was to succumb to the second new ball, taken just minutes before the close.

'Richard was about a yard and a half quicker with the new cherry,' said Oxlade. 'He'd taken only one wicket all day, as the crowd regularly reminded him, and he hit me in the ribs with a short one.

'I was expecting a yorker the second time around [but] he let go with another short ball. I saw it, tried to sway out of the way, and it hit me in the head and down I went. My head was swimming. I was conscious but I just couldn't get up. I had this beaut black eye for days.'

Always a patient batsman, Oxlade had taken six hours to make 95, but was so badly hurt he could not return the following day. Looking back, he says he was lucky enough to play four matches against visiting international sides, and regards the games as the highlights of his 20-year career.

p

||||||||||||

PARTY ANIMAL

Not only was David Boon a damn fine cricketer, he was the ultimate party animal, and still holds the record for downing the most cans of beer (43) on an international flight (from Tullamarine to Heathrow in 1989).

PATSY THE FUNSTER

Englishman Elias Henry 'Patsy' Hendren was a great funster and always enjoyed a friendly rapport with the barrackers in Australia. At Geelong one day, while chasing a ball to the boundary, Patsy retrieved an apple and threw it one-bounce in to the wicketkeeper. There it burst, much to the merriment of all except the stand-in captain, the normally affable Rockley Wilson. Despite the match being of little consequence, Wilson felt Hendren was being a little too flippant.

In a game against Victoria, Patsy celebrated his thirty-second birthday with an innings of 271. At an average of almost 90 runs per session, his square-of-the-wicket strokeplay was particularly masterful. Earlier in the tour, also against the Victorians, he'd made an unbeaten 106.

Hendren made three visits down-under, his last in his fortieth year, in 1928–29. Only the legendary Jack Hobbs amassed more centuries in English first-class cricket. Hendren also played football for his country, in the 1919 Victory International.

PAYING THE PRICE

Terry Jenner still goes to his local TAB in beachside Adelaide for a flutter. Like thousands of Australians, he loves a bet. Always has; always will. The fact that he has served time for a gambling addiction is immaterial. He has a second chance at life and a totally fresh set of priorities.

Thirty years ago, Jenner was a member of Australia's globetrotting champion cricket team, intent on partying as hard as he played, not knowing if he truly belonged or when it would all end. Seeing another high-profile Australian cricketer cash in his match cheque at an illegal gambling joint and win, Jenner followed suit. Within an hour, he had lost the lot.

Most of the money Jenner earned during his topsy-turvy career was squandered. He retired just before the advent of World Series Cricket and was bitter at missing his chance at the most lucrative cricket monies of his life. A $5000 cheque to coach an Adelaide suburban club was cashed in at the races, and most left with the bagman. Jenner says the sinking feeling he experienced when he realised the horse he'd backed couldn't win was all too familiar. In the end, he lost all self-control. Winning or losing was immaterial. He'd gamble until he had nothing left.

Jenner's sports store went bankrupt within six months of opening and, so desperate was he to meet his debts, he buried himself in volleys of deceit and lies. He was selling tow bars to the car industry when a car-yard manager approached him, recognised him as the ex-cricketer and asked, 'What's Terry Jenner doing selling tow bars?'

'Everyone's got to make a living, mate.'

The manager asked Jenner how much he was earning a week.

'$200.'

The manager said he needed a new salesman and $200 would be Jenner's minimum wage if he came to work for him. What's more, he'd be on a bonus for every car sold. Jenner learnt quickly and, some weeks, took home close to $1000. But none was ever banked, as he plunged further and further into the mire.

He was on the run from family and friends, and embezzled money to pay his debts. Before sentencing him to six-and-a-half years' imprisonment, the judge called him a parasite on society and beyond rehabilitation. Few high-profile sportsmen had fallen as hard.

As unpalatable and degrading as the prison system was, Jenner says it was also his saviour. His priorities shifted. No longer was his gambling all-important. It was family that counted. The support of his cricket mates, especially ex-Test captain Ian Chappell, was an enormous boost. Due to good behaviour, his term was reduced to 18 months in prison and a further six months on home detention.

The first time Chappell visited Jenner in prison, Jenner broke down, saying he'd disgraced not only himself but all his old teammates. Chappell had never considered his mate a criminal; he needed help, like anyone else with an illness. Chappell feared Jenner's spirits were so low he may attempt suicide.

'Ian,' said Jenner, 'we had to fill in a list of questions on arrival. I said yes to the first 19 and no to the last.' (The twentieth question was whether the prisoner would consider suicide.)

While some found excuses not to visit, Chappell never did. In the foreword to Jenner's autobiography, *T.J. Over the Top*, Chappell writes, 'Once a captain, always a captain.' And when Jenner had served his time, Chappell encouraged him to look people in the eye, something that is shunned in prisons.

Chappell knew of the specialist coaching Jenner had

been doing while on parole. When Jenner's star pupil, Shane Warne, first made the Australian team, it was Chappell who asked him to consider a request from the ABC's Neville Oliver to talk about Warne on radio.

'C'mon, you've got nothing to lose,' he said.

'Okay, I'll see you there [at the ABC studio],' said Jenner. 'I'm walking around the back.'

'Bugger that!' said Chappell. 'You've done your time. You've paid your price. You're going to walk around with me, with your head high.'

It was my privilege to work with Terry on his life story, the good and the bad. One night, well past midnight, he had tears streaming down his cheeks as he recalled the walkout of his wife and how close he felt he'd come to losing his daughter, too. Several times he stopped, hardly daring to tread further, before taking a breath and going again.

Jenner told me at the start of the project that he wanted *T.J. Over the Top* to be the best book I'd ever written. It was.

PEERLESS IN CLOSE

No wonder the Chappell brothers (Ian, Greg and Trevor all played for Australia) were peerless in the slips. From the time they could walk, their father, Martin, tossed them balls.

'And never mind *soft* balls,' said Ian. 'They were cricket balls. He'd walk around and suddenly, out of the blue, this cricket ball would be coming at you. We all learnt to be alert. There was no choice but to react . . . and react fast!'

THE PEOPLE'S CHAMPION

Sent to Siberia while still in his prime, Dean Jones hated life amongst the second-stringers. Frustrated by his continuing non-selection and yearning for home, he cracked in faraway South Africa, announcing his international exit. And no amount of back-pedalling, mega-scoring or popular pressure in his home town of Melbourne could convince the national selectors that Victoria's best cricketer was anything but retired.

Proud, brash and opinionated, Jones could certainly play. But, in the inner sanctum, his acceptance levels had plummeted, prompting speculation he'd been dropped for reasons other than cricket. Even the Victorian hierachy lost faith, forcing him into a teary retirement.

'BRING BACK DEANO' banners are still seen at the MCG – testimony to the respect earned by 'The Ledge' ('The Legend', a nickname Jones coined himself).

PETER THE PRODIGY

Dropped six times before he'd played even 15 Tests, burly Queenslander Peter Burge was contemplating a job outside cricket, as the Brisbane accountancy firm for which he was working kept docking his pay when he had to attend practice. Burge had even penned a letter refusing his invitation to tour India and Pakistan in 1959–60, when a more generous employer emerged to rejuvenate his career both on and off the field.

The son of Jack Burge, a former prominent Queensland administrator, Burge was a schoolboy star, notching his first century as a nine-year-old and, at 13, hitting six centuries, a double-century and a 99 in 10 innings.

His Queensland and Test teammate Peter Allan said Burge's forearms were so massive that his bat looked like a matchstick. All four of his Test centuries came against England. He thrived on the cut and thrust of Ashes battles and was much-loved among teammates for his fearless approach.

When Burge died in 2001, former teammate Bill

Lawry said, 'If you had a son, you'd like him to be like Peter Burge.'

PREMIERSHIP SPECIALIST

Warrnambool veteran Trevor McKenzie's record of 15 A-grade premierships with Nestles is unsurpassed among current players in country Victoria. His former coach, Western Districts stalwart Ian 'Lefty' Wright, also played in 15 premierships. McKenzie thought he had the record well covered in the early nineties, with Nestles continuing to dominate in Warrnambool.

'I actually caught Lefty in 1992 and thought I had a few good years left, only for us to lose six grand finals in a row,' said McKenzie. 'It was a record which wasn't meant to be broken. We'd won practically every year, too, up until then.'

In an under-16 grand final, McKenzie once took all 10 wickets in an innings. In 1983, as first-time captain of the first XI, he took nine for 40 on a hard wicket against West Warrnambool. He was also captain of the club's A-grade premiership treble from 1983–85.

As accurate a leg-spinner as could be found in country Victoria in the 1980s and 1990s, McKenzie's record of more than 300 A-grade games and 700-plus wickets rightly won him a place in the Victorian country's all-star XI of the nineties.

PRICKLE PALACE

Mrs Daphney Bichel, wife for 47 years of Ipswich legend Don Bichel, laughs when she recalls her late husband's nickname.

'His mates called him "Spud Hands", as he didn't drop too many in the field,' she said. 'One day, though, at Ipswich, one of the local bowlers, John Verrankamp, had nine wickets and Don put down the tenth. Johnny never let Don forget it.

'Another time, at Goondiwindi, there were so many prickles growing in the outfield [that] Don and the rest of them fielded with plastic bags to protect their hands!'

PRINCELY BEGINNINGS

Long-stop was an important position, even at Test cricket level, until the arrival of South Melbourne genius Jack Blackham. He stood over the stumps to even the fastest of bowlers, 'the Demon' Fred Spofforth included. Blackham had begun his career in Carlton's second XI but, having been blocked in his bid to play regular senior cricket, he accepted an invitation to transfer to South via its captain, the highly influential John Conway. He performed so brilliantly in the inaugural Test match (Melbourne, 1876–77), that he was presented with a diamond ring and a gold medal by the Victorian Cricket Association.

PRODUCING WHEN IT COUNTED

For all his outward serenity, Paul Reiffel, Australia's No. 1 all-rounder of the late nineties, says he was like a duck – apparently cruising on top of the water while actually paddling madly beneath it.

'I always had to work to make teams. Nothing was presented to me easily,' he said.

Asked to rate his all-time favourite moment, he opted for Jamaica '95, when Australia clinched the World Championship after almost two decades of West Indian domination. West Indian hopes of saving their title were dashed on the penultimate evening, when Reiffel claimed three wickets in the burst of his life: Richie Richardson caught and bowled; Stuart Williams bowled; and, the peach of all wickets, Brian Lara lbw to Reiffel's signature ball, the off-cutter.

'Just to be part of that team was something very special, and even more satisfying to play the role I did,' he said.

According to cricket legend and current Australian Test selector Allan Border, Reiffel was one of those unsung heroes you loved to have in your side, as they invariably produced when it counted.

'PUT TRIBE ON!'

One of the first spin bowlers selected for Australia after World War II was left-arm wrist-spinner George Tribe. His local club was North Melbourne, situated in the heart of blue-collar territory, directly opposite the Kensington railyards.

Often after work on a Saturday, a stream of colourful characters would walk across from the yards into the Arden Street ground and barrack . . . hard. The loudest by far was 'Rooster' O'Connor, a rough-as butcher's assistant who loved North and was fiercely loyal to the players, especially Tribe. North was playing Northcote at home this day and, unbeknown to Rooster, George had a bad arm and was being nursed through by his captain, Bob Dempster.

Rooster kept on bellowing, 'Put Tribe on!' Dempster finally threw the ball to Tribe who, during an over consisting mainly of long hops, was dispatched all around the ground. Rooster yelled out again, 'Take this imposter off and put Tribe on!'

q

|||||||||||||

QUADRUPLE CENTURION

Few in Australian country cricket circles possessed as straight and broad a bat as Keith Savage. He was one of the Riverina's most celebrated sportsmen and famous for amassing a record-equalling 408 in the 1950–51 Griffith district season. In a year in which he shared in three consecutive triple-century opening stands, Savage made eight centuries in as many matches. He thanks his grandmother, Roberta, for helping nurture a rock-solid technique.

'She was very keen on cricket and had six sons, including my dad [Graham], who all played,' said Savage. 'We had a spare house on the farm and she'd get me over there in the evenings. There was a corridor with the lino tacked down and she would have me swinging the bat straight. One night, she followed through with a little too much gusto and bashed the globe. I said to her, "We'll have to appeal against the light now, Grandma!"'

Pint-sized at 155 cm (5'2"), Savage had an insatiable appetite for runs. In all, he made 35 centuries. He amassed 1000 runs or more six times in a Riverina season. Twice, he passed 2000 runs. His monumental 408 came in a semifinal in Griffith. Incredibly, it took just six hours, and included 66 fours but not even one six.

'My team, Griffith CYMs, were playing the Griffith Teachers. We batted first and made 877, including five century-partnerships,' he said. 'I can't remember giving a chance, but I was beaten by a beautiful ball at about 40, which cut back from outside the off stump and only just missed the leg stump. I was only about 21 and pretty fit from working on the [family's orange] farm and playing a lot of tennis as well. We played half-days back then, on malthoid.'

Asked if his teammates made a particular fuss after his quadruple century, he said, 'No . . . but we had a bit of a party after we won the final the following week.'

Did Savage feel like giving someone else a hit at any stage during that innings?

'No, I thought it was my responsibility to keep going. We had a good side, but you never know what can happen. [In a previous match] I'd thrown my innings away, having made 200-odd, and we lost. As it was, they got close to 400 in reply. It was a high-scoring game all right.'

When Savage made eight centuries in a row, he was invited to play in Adelaide and even England.

'In those days, the money was not there. Being a farmer, you stick to the farm,' he said.

Savage was a leading member of Leeton's O'Farrell Cup team, which won 23 matches in a row under the captaincy of Derek Rogers in 1967 and 1968. Savage played in 21 of the matches.

Another of his finest moments came in 1951, when he was selected for NSW Country against City. Representing the Murrumbidgee Country Week team in Sydney that season, he made more than 400 runs, at an average approaching 100.

His A-grade career aggregate was 16 500 and career average 58. In 1951, he shared in three consecutive triple-century opening stands with Alan Davidson's uncle, Arthur Clifton, for Yoogali in Griffith. The stands were worth 300, 305 and 321, and are probably unequalled in any standard of city or bush cricket. (Clifton also

> ## HIGHEST INNINGS IN AUSTRALIAN COUNTRY CRICKET
>
> 408 Tom Patton, 1913–14
> (Buffalo River, Gapstead Association, Victoria)
> 408 Keith Savage, 1950–51
> (Griffith CYM, Griffith District Cricket
> Association, NSW)
> 406 Frank Henderson, 1929–30
> (Leeton, Leeton District Cricket Association, NSW)
> 393 H. Burgoyne, 1939–40
> (Moss Vale, Old Park-Moss Vale Association, NSW)

took more than 1000 wickets for Yoogali and played at first-grade level in Sydney.)

SEE: WAGGA WAGGA RICHES, PAGE 219

QUICK ENOUGH FOR ME

When it came to collecting premierships, few had a happier knack of being in the right place at the right time than Wangaratta's Peter Tossol. At Thornton Cricket Club alone, Tossol was part of 10 flags in 11 years, including six in his six years as captain. Also a star footballer, Tossol says he was blessed to have had such a happy association with sport, ever since his days as a boarder at Assumption College where he was deputy cricket captain behind international-to-be Simon O'Donnell.

'I wasn't good enough to make it as a top-line footballer and cricketer,' he says, 'but I worked hard at getting the most out of my ability.'

Tossol *was* good enough to play League football with Melbourne and to make 70-odd against a West

Indian touring team that included Malcolm Marshall, Joel Garner and a young Courtney Walsh. He says that, these days, choices have to be made between cricket and football if young players are truly to progress to elite levels.

A left-hander, his career-high of 210 came in a semi final for Thornton against Waratahs at Alexandra. He also made a double-century, twice, in grand finals in the Alexandra-Mansfield Cricket Association.

Tossol was a member of six Victorian country championship squads. He was an All-Australian one memorable summer, the year the Australian country side defeated a New South Wales XI that included Test bowling trio Geoff Lawson, Mike Whitney and Murray Bennett.

Like one of his best mates, Geoff 'Flops' Phillips from Tatyoon, Tossol says he never worried about a helmet, even against the West Indian expressmen when they came to Wangaratta for a one-dayer in the mid-eighties.

'They had a pretty fair team on paper, including all their fast bowlers. I don't think too many of them were going full bore, but Courtney Walsh was certainly quick enough for me. I had a much-worn favourite pair of gloves, without too much padding. At one stage, he struck me on the hand. I found out later it was broken.'

QUICK FROM NINETEEN YARDS

Len Pascoe loved to bowl short. It didn't matter who was on strike. Anyone with a bat in their hands was fair game, he reckoned. Testing out Australian captain Greg Chappell with a bouncer one day in a Sheffield Shield game in Sydney, he watched in horror as Chappell's attempted pull shot miscued, just out of reach at mid-on. As Chappell ran a single and surveyed the bottom end of his bat, Pascoe let forth, 'Thought you could hook.'

'Thought you could bowl fast,' came the reply.

The next time Chappell was on strike, Pascoe steamed in, overstepped and sent one past his nose. Staring at him from mid-pitch, with eyes flaming, Pascoe asked, 'Fast enough?'

'Yes thank you, Lenny. But can you do it from 22 yards?'

THE QUICKEST SINCE '38

It was a wartime charity match at Lord's between an England XI and the Dominions, and Denis Compton was enjoying the hit-out just as much as the thousands of fans who had assembled.

'Luck was smiling upon me that day and I felt set for a big score,' Compton said. 'Finally, the ball was thrown to a tall, brushed-back-haired fellow who had been racing around the boundary like a young gazelle, and whose gigantic throws had drawn whistles of admiration from the crowd. He was the fifth bowling change.'

Not knowing what to expect, Compton turned to the 'keeper, Stan Sismey, for an indication.

'Oh, he's not really a bowler,' said Sismey. 'I expect he wants a bit of exercise, but you might find him a bit quick.'

'A bit quick?' remembers Compton. 'He took only a short run but, when he let the ball go, my hair nearly stood up on end. It was the fastest ball bowled to me since I'd played against Ernie McCormick and the 1938 Australians! Such was my introduction to Keith Miller.'

QUITE A FEAT

Michael Cox, 17, took five wickets in five balls for Epping's second XI against Mill Park in Diamond Valley

(Melbourne suburban) cricket in 2005. Bowling first change on a synthetic wicket, his figures were 7-4-16-7. His wickets were bowled, lbw, bowled, bowled, bowled and caught. His last wicket was in a fresh over.

r

||||||||||||

RAISED ON SPORT

Few champions are as modest as Belinda Clark, the Bradman of women cricketers, who keeps much of her memorabilia and old pictures in boxes in the roof of her inner-Melbourne house. Naturally drawn to the game as a young, sports-mad girl growing up in Newcastle, Clark loved attending matches at the Newcastle No. 1, or catching the train south past the delightfully named Woy Woy and the picturesque Hawkesbury River all the way into Sydney, to watch a Test or a one-dayer. In 1990–91, she achieved the rare distinction of making her state, one-day international *and* Test debuts in the same season. And in 2004–05, she became the first woman to play 100 one-day internationals.

'My upbringing was based around sport,' she said. 'On school holidays, you'd go and play in a tennis tournament. You wouldn't just be sitting around. My brother and two sisters were the same. They all played sport, too. I'd ride my brother's hand-me-down pushbike to events on a Saturday, from one venue to another: hockey to tennis to cricket. It was nothing for us to play three different sports on the same day. They were great times.'

There's much of her uncomplicated childhood that Clark would love to rekindle, like the vanilla thick shakes and the sausage rolls she and her sisters would devour in between Saturday sporting events. But, she says, any such indulgences will need to wait until she's well and truly retired!

READY TO RUMBLE

It's not every day that a touring captain threatens to 'drop' his vice-captain. But Ian Johnson was furious and, having been an amateur boxer before the war, he was ready to rumble. The Australians led the series 2-0 coming to Bridgetown (fourth Test, 1955) and were in a formidable position. They'd made 668 on a belter of a wicket, before quickly dismissing two of the West Indies' finest, a young Garry Sobers and an in-form Clyde Walcott. Everton Weekes and Frank Worrell were mounting some opposition, however, and Johnson – looking for another breakthrough – asked his deputy, the mercurial Keith Miller, to bowl two or three really fast overs to see if he could expose the middle order.

'I knew Ray Lindwall took an over or two to warm up, but Keith could slip into it straight away,' said Johnson, in an interview with Robert Coleman, author of *Seasons in the Sun*. 'So I told him I wanted him to come on next over.

'"Be buggered," Keith said to me. "I'm not coming on. It's no good for me, this. I don't want to bowl here."'

Johnson couldn't believe it. He didn't know what to say.

'At the end of the over, I walked down one side of the wicket,' Johnson continued. 'Keith was on the other and I threw the ball to him. I told him that he was bowling, and to throw the ball back to me if he had the guts.

'He mumbled and moaned, and he went on and bowled half-pace. There was a strong crosswind blowing and he got a big out-curve and did in fact pick up a couple of wickets [two in an over].

'I kept him on for another three or four overs and they woke up to the big out-curl. I told him to give us some fast stuff, or he'd be off.

'"I'm doing all right."'

'So I brought Ray Lindwall back. He had a catch dropped in his first over, before the West Indian pair [of Denis Atkinson and Clairmonte Depeiza] added almost 350 for the seventh wicket.

'Having not wanted to bowl in the first place, Keith put on a bit of an act when he was taken off. We got into the dressing-room [with the West Indies 6/187] and Keith Butler, from *The* [Adelaide] *Advertiser* came up and asked what was happening. Keith told him that I couldn't captain a team of bloody schoolboys.

'I had to go to a show that night and had my own car. As we were leaving, Keith said, "I'm going now. I'm going back with the boys."

'"No you're not," I said. "You're coming back with me. We're going to have a talk."

'He hopped in the car and I said to him, "That was a dirty trick you pulled today. I didn't like it."

'"Well," he said, "you don't like being taken off when you're getting wickets, do you?"

'I told him that if he ever did it again, I'd drop him, in front of the team. There was a pause.

'"You'd do it, too, wouldn't you?" he said.

'"You know bloody well I would."

'"Arr," he said, "let's forget it. Shake hands." We did and he was as good as gold after that. We were good mates and stayed that way. Never again did Keith let me down when he was needed.'

REBUKED BY THE DON

Australia's twelfth man in three Tests in the early sixties, Jack Potter, was feeling rather pleased with himself. He'd just run out the champion Springbok Eddie Barlow with a direct hit (Melbourne, 1963). Back in the Australian rooms, he smiled as he walked past Sir Donald Bradman.

'But instead of any congratulations, the Don told me how I'd mucked up the series by running out their best player!' Potter said. 'I'm sure it was said in jest, but I've never forgotten it.'

Potter said he'd simply got lucky. Barlow had taken a quick single to midwicket, only for the ball to conveniently jump right into his hands.

'There was a run there nine times out of 10. It was my first time in the team and I was only on for about three or four overs, substituting for Garth [Graham] McKenzie.

'I was also twelfth man twice in England in 1964. I was happy just to be in the [touring squad of] 17, let alone the XII. The guys I played with were just so good. I thought I had some sort of chance [of playing] early in the tour, as Peter Burge was out of form. But he made that great 160 [in the third Test] at Leeds, which helped

AUSTRALIAN TWELFTH MEN NEVER TO PLAY A TEST

Geoff Davies (NSW)	1968–69
Shaun Graf (Vic.)	1980–81
Les Hill (SA)	1907–08
Syd Hird (NSW)	1932–33
Jock Irvine (WA)	1969–70
Col McKenzie (Vic.)	1907–08
Ian McLachlan (SA)	1962–63
Les Poidevin (NSW)	1901–02
Jack Potter (Vic.)	1963–64 & 1964
Ian Quick (Vic.)	1961
Bert Tobin (SA)	1932–33
Sam Trimble (Qld)	1964–65
'Gar' Waddy (NSW)	1907–08

us win with more than a day to spare. Once again, the selectors were proved right.

'In 1980, for the Centenary Test in England, everyone who had played a Test in England was invited back. I asked what the criteria were, but it turned out the Australian Cricket Board didn't recognise the twelfth men. I didn't get a trip.'

'RED . . . YOU'RE IN!'

Having made a duck in the first innings, Bob Simpson was back at the crease in the second when Ian Redpath, next man in, answered a call of nature. Lightning surely couldn't strike twice in the same match.

But it did. Simpson duly fell again, to the young Warwickshire expressman David Brown – and again without scoring.

'Are you there, Red?' came the call.

No answer.

'Red . . . you're in!'

Still no answer. The only man with his pads on in the Lord's dressing-room was wicketkeeper Barry Jarman. Out he went and so dominated that he joined the elite club of those to score a ton at the home of cricket.

RED-LETTER DAY

The sports-mad Gippsland town of Leongatha was all but afloat the day the touring MCC team arrived for its match against a Victorian country XI in high spring, 1978. As the two captains, Bob Willis and Leongatha's own Al Sperling, looked at the ever-so-green turf wicket, just laid, Willis turned to Sperling.

'I know you've put a lot of work into the day, but you can't control the rain. Tell you what, if we can bat first, we'll play.'

Sperling nodded and said, 'You can bat for four days if you want to. We've got 5000 people here.'

Eighteen wickets were to fall for less than 200 runs on the greentop, with the country XI making just 59. But it was still a red-letter day for Sperling, the La Trobe Valley's ultimate cricket legend who played for 40 seasons.

A RICH HERITAGE

When 12-year-old Mick Rantall took seven for 11 in his very first open-age game for Jancourt East, the locals at Cobden nodded wisely and talked of the rich Rantall sporting heritage. The Rantall name is legend in western Victoria. Mick's cousin, John, was one of the greats of the Victorian Football League throughout the sixties and seventies. And his father, Albert, was a most competitive bowling all-rounder, who'd let nothing stand in the way of his Saturday afternoon cricket. One day at Jancourt, a four-foot brown snake slithered towards gully, much to the consternation of the catching ring. Albert's answer was to use his Gray-Nicolls Scoop to whack the unwanted visitor where it hurts, dispose of it over the fence and calmly resume batting.

RING-INS (I)

In his first game for more than a year for suburban Melbourne club Mill Park, 26-year-old Luke Petersen made 447 not out, all on one Sunday afternoon against South Morang (2001–02).

'I only played because the fifth XI boys were short,' said Peterson, who struck 37 sixes and 38 fours after coming in at No. 3. He gave three chances, including one that was fumbled and went over the rope for six, à la the infamous Paul Reiffel miss of Lance Klusener during the '99 World Cup semifinal at Old Trafford.

Ironically, Luke's only previous open-age century was for South Morang against Mill Park.

RING-INS (II)

Closer examination of the Thames Valley Gents' XI saw one 'S. Waugh' down to bat at No. 4. I was on tour with the Australian Crusaders in '87 and we were drawn to play at Teddington in one of the feature matches. Not only did our opponents include Waugh, but also his NSW teammates, Brad McNamara and David Gilbert.

Finding myself bowling in tandem with Paul Jackson, the Richmond and Victorian finger-spinner, I ignored the champagne and other goodies on offer during an extended lunchbreak so I could be at my best immediately afterwards.

'This could be Waugh or Piesse,' said our ever-genial 'keeper Mark Foster, as Waugh rechecked his guard.

Six balls later I knew that writing, rather than leg-breaks, would be by far the wiser career choice. Not only did balls one and three go for six, but so did balls five and six! And, in between, Waugh helped himself to boundaries square of the wicket. My analysis: 6 4 6 4 6 6 (32 from one over)! Australia's captain-to-be made 90 in about 45 minutes and walked off to a standing ovation.

RULES ARE RULES

Before being allowed to join the team en route to Australia, members of the 1932–33 English touring team had to agree to the following:

Flying is forbidden. Players must not take part in games or sport that might endanger life or limb; and players must not write for, or give interviews to, the press.

Ship and hotel behaviour also had to be exemplary:

*The players will dine in the public rooms, the accommo-
dation for all [professionals and amateurs] will be the
same and they will travel together.*

RUNNING LATE

When Arthur Mailey wasn't spinning luxuriant, loopy leg-
spinners high into the air, he could be found in a corner,
pencil in hand, practising his cartooning. He had a brace
of wonderful books and booklets published, a set of which
is now highly collectible.

The 1921 Australians were playing Western Province
at Cape Town. With only a few wickets down, Mailey
had decided to stay at the team's lodgings to work on
some cartoons, and would come to the ground later. But
when he heard that there had been a collapse, and not
wanting to incur a fine for being late, he jumped on a
train. As it was going by the ground, he realised that the
second-last pair was in.

One of the Australians caught in the collapse, Hunter
'Stork' Hendry, was an eyewitness to the rapidity with
which Mailey changed. 'He only had time to pull his
white trousers over his suit ones and drag a shirt over his
street one and boots over ordinary socks, with the help
of pals to save the fine!'

While Mailey was to make only five with the bat, he
did take 11 wickets for the match.

S

||||||||||||

SECOND-CHANCE HEROES

Eleven players who have made significant contributions after swapping states, in batting order:

1. **Bill Brown**
   Toowoomba-born, he made three tours to England: one as a NSW player and two as a Queenslander.
2. **Jack Badcock**
   The pocket-sized right-hander from the Tasmanian bush fought his way into Australia's top six and made the 1938 tour to England, having shifted to Adelaide.
3. **Don Bradman (captain)**
   A business career in stockbroking caused the record-breaker to cross from NSW to South Australia in the mid-thirties.
4. **Greg Chappell**
   After seven seasons in his native Adelaide, he transferred to Queensland in 1973 and, soon afterwards, captained Australia.
5. **Allan Border**
   Originally from Mosman and the grittiest of batsmen, he played in Queensland's inaugural Sheffield Shield title success, aged 40.
6. **Keith Miller**
   Married his American-born wife, Peg, and shifted to Sydney in 1947, having learned the game in Melbourne. He captained NSW and was vice-captain of Australia.

7. **Adam Gilchrist**
   Forged a remarkable career for WA and Australia after leaving his native NSW. He has four of the five quickest Test centuries by an Australian.
8. **Colin Miller**
   Originally from Melbourne's unfashionable west, his career took off in Tasmania when he started to combine his medium-pace swingers with his late-developing off-breaks.
9. **Jeff Thomson**
   Originally a NSW Test player, he was lured to Brisbane in a huge marketing deal. Among the elite group of Australians to take 200 Test wickets.
10. **Clarrie Grimmett**
    New Zealand-born, he played at Sheffield Shield level in Victoria before thriving on the new No. 1 spinning responsibility granted him by Vic Richardson in Adelaide.
11. **Rodney Hogg**
    His career exploded on his shift from Melbourne to Adelaide. No one will ever forget his career-best Ashes summer: 41 wickets at 12.75 in 1978–79.

SECRETS OF SUCCESS

Bobby Simpson had a novel way of taking slips catches.

'I used to let them hit me at a certain height, where you couldn't always get your hands right,' he said. 'I always found the hardest catch was the one straight at you. I tended to try and take it on the inside. Every now and then they came a bit quick to do it, so I'd let it hit my chest and then wrap my arms around it. I thought it was the safest way.'

With 110 catches in 62 Tests, Simpson remains one of Australia's finest slippers.

SEEING DOUBLE AT SABINA

It was at Sabina Park, Jamaica, in '73 that Max 'Tangles' Walker found out what it was really like to drink full-strength rum. He'd just dismissed local hero Lawrence Rowe and was resting, down on the fine-leg fence. Life in the Caribbean was looking pretty good when one of the fans yelled, 'Hey, Wocker! Wocker, you bowl another ball like that, maan, and you can have my wife!'

Tangles turned to see a man accompanied by a short, well-rounded woman with a toothy grin. She was laughing like a hyena. Smiling at his new-found mate and nodding politely to his laughing lady, Walker said thanks and that he was thoroughly appreciative of the offer. But, he explained, he'd better stay focused on the cricket, as that was why he was there.

A little later, after another wicket, the man again leaned over the fence. 'Hey, Wocker! Wocker, you hot, maan? You hot?'

Tangles admitted that he was, and gratefully took a large paper cup thrust at him. About halfway through the cup, he realised that what he'd thought was Coca-Cola wasn't anything of the sort. In fact, if there was any Coke in it, it was only a smidgin. Basically, he was drinking 100 per cent proof rum.

Everyone was delighted and, trying to hide his agony, Tangles offered a smile and dramatically grabbed at his throat, bringing even more cheers from the crowd. He reckons he saw double next time he ran in to bowl, and it took several litres of water at the drinks break to re-find his equilibrium.

SEEING THE FUNNY SIDE

Only Lindsay Hassett could have got away with it. Having dropped Cyril Washbrook twice from Ray Lindwall's bowling at long leg (Old Trafford, 1948), he borrowed a policeman's hat and, holding it in front of him like a giant cup, told Lindwall he was ready for a third attempt!

SELECTION SQUABBLES

The time Tasmania's Ken Burn was chosen as the deputy wicketkeeper behind 'The Prince' of 'keepers, Jack Blackham, remains one of the worst selection blunders ever. Victoria's Jack Harry had been earmarked for the job, only to be passed over in a squabble between Victorian and NSW interests. As a compromise, the Tasmanian was chosen. But, on arrival in Adelaide to board the ship taking the team to the mother country, Burn declared, 'Well, here I am, but I've never kept wickets in my life!'

He was to play the only two Tests of his career on tour, batting at No. 10 and No. 11 on debut at Lord's, and No. 6 and opening at The Oval. In all first-class cricket, he averaged 30, with two centuries.

SERIES OF A LIFETIME

Few were braver than Melbourne-born Colin McDonald, who wore more bruises than any other Australian opener in history. And in his day there were no helmets or thigh guards; even the opening batsmen went in with nothing more elaborate than a couple of reinforcing hankies stuffed into a hip pocket. Rated the world's No. 1 batsman in 1959, after amassing 519 runs in five Ashes Tests against Peter May's touring MCC, McDonald made three half-centuries in a row, before finishing the series with 170 in Adelaide and 184 in Melbourne.

'It was the thrill of a lifetime,' he said. 'It was the first time I'd made a century against England and to make another in the very next Test, on my home ground, was

The 1946–47 Victorians, resplendent in their sports coats and trousers from
Roger David stores in Melbourne.
BACK, from left: Sam Loxton, Fred Freer, Gordon Tamblyn, Doug Ring, Keith
Miller, Bill Johnston, Ken Meuleman.
FRONT: Ian Johnson, George Tribe, Merv Harvey, Lindsay Hassett
(captain), Ben Barnett.

Bill Brown captained Australia for just eight hours in Wellington in 1945–46. The touring team was the first to fly overseas, with the trans-Tasman crossing taking nine hours!
BACK, from left: W. Watts (scorer), Don Tallon, Keith Miller, Bill O'Reilly (vice-captain), Ernie Toshack, Bruce Dooland, Ron Hamence, E. C. Yeomans (manager).
FRONT: Ian Johnson, Col McCool, Lindsay Hassett, Bill Brown (captain), Sid Barnes, Ken Meuleman, Ray Lindwall.

Keith Miller made a habit of lighting up any room he entered. Here, the charismatic superstar of Australian sport is pictured (left) at the tour opener at East Molesey in 1953, with Lindsay Hassett and the Duke of Edinburgh.

Richie Benaud entered big cricket just as Don Bradman was leaving it. One of his few regrets is never to have bowled to the Don.

The 1955 Australian team on their tour of the West Indies. BACK, from left: Les Favell, Len Maddocks, Jack Hill, Ron Archer, J. Burge (manager), Peter Burge, Alan Davidson, Billy Watson, Colin McDonald. FRONT: Neil Harvey, Bill Johnston, Arthur Morris, Ian Johnson (captain), Keith Miller, Ray Lindwall, Richie Benaud, Gil Langley. A furious Johnson threatened to punch Miller during the fourth Test when Miller refused to bowl fast.

Ian Redpath and Tom Veivers after winning the Test at Cape Town, 1966–67.

Ex-teammates, national selectors and bosom buddies on and off the field, Sam Loxton (left) and Neil Harvey (centre), with fellow selector Phil Ridings. 'I'm more or less a father to him,' Loxton once said of Harvey.

The volatile Rodney Hogg loses it, momentarily, after taking a wicket in Trinidad in 1984. His retreating teammate is Australia's captain, Kim Hughes.

Ray Titus/Cricketer magazine

Les Favell's last innings, Old South Australia v. Old Victoria, Adelaide, 1986–87. He made a rapid-fire dozen.

Mike Whitney's finest moment in cricket was surviving an over from Richard
Hadlee in the 1987–88 Melbourne Test.

CRICKETER MAGAZINE

Terry Alderman, just seconds after being felled by a spectator at the WACA
Ground in 1982–83.

JOHN CAMPBELL/THE WEST AUSTRALIAN

Ian Botham leaps for joy as Australia falls just a boundary short of victory in the 1982–83 Christmas Test in Melbourne. Allan Border and Jeff Thomson added 70 for the last wicket in one of the great stands.

CRICKETER MAGAZINE

very satisfying. Funnily enough, in Adelaide, the very first ball I faced from Brian Statham went right through me and only just cleared the middle stump. I could have easily been out for nought and wouldn't have had such a great season.'

McDonald's career had swung around since 1953 when Australia's captain, Lindsay Hassett, had told him he was too front-on. 'Lindsay cured me,' he said, 'and made me a better player.'

SETTLING THE NERVES

Having been welcomed to the wicket by Keith Miller, Ashes debutant Neil Harvey watched in amazement as Miller lifted Jim Laker for two sixes during his opening over of the 1948 Old Trafford Test.

'It helped settle my nerves,' Harvey said. 'I thought to myself that this game is not so hard after all.'

Harvey went on to make 112 and there was no more-celebrated debut Test century until Michael Clarke's 151 against India (Bangalore, 2004).

SHE MISSED HIS ENTIRE CAREER

It remains one of the most famous first-ball ducks of all – and the only time prominent Melburnian doctor Roy Park ever did play for Australia. Originally named as twelfth man for the Melbourne Test of 1920–21, Park took his place in the side when Charles Macartney withdrew because of illness. His wife dropped her knitting just as Park faced the first ball and, as she was bending down to pick it up, Park's stumps were shattered by another first-gamer, England's Harry Howell.

Park's son-in-law was Ian Johnson and, years later, he confirmed that Park had been up all the night before, attending a difficult birth.

'He didn't want to say a word about it at the time. He didn't want to make any excuses,' said Johnson.

Johnson remembers bowling to Park in his forties and thinking, 'This bloke's a bit hard to get out!'

Park's first-class average bordered on 40. He was also a talented footballer, representing the University and Melbourne clubs.

SHOAIB THE QUICKEST

With more than 20 000 first-class runs and a career average of 50, batting at No. 3 and No. 4, Queenslander Stuart Law is well qualified to rate the fastest bowlers of his era. On their day, he said Merv Hughes and Carl Rackemann were near express, but no one compared with Pakistan's Shoaib Akhtar.

'When he [Akhtar] first came out here in '99, he was fearsome in full flight,' said Law. 'It was the only time I've ever heard the ball whistling at me on the way down.'

SHOOTING STAR

Of Bob Massie's astonishing 16-wicket Test debut in 1972, his pace partner Dennis Lillee said, 'It was as good as I'd seen anyone bowl. I still bowled pretty well but, compared with Bob, I was probably pretty ordinary. It was his match. He's a great guy and thoroughly deserved his success.' Only once before had Massie returned anything like those figures – a nine-for, representing Mount Lawley High against Kent Street High (a team that included fellow teenager Rodney Marsh).

The accolades for 25-year-old Massie included 'Wisden Cricketer of the Year' but, amazingly, he was to play just two more Tests for Australia before disappearing almost completely, having lost his ability to bowl his signature outswinger.

THE SHOT OF HIS LIFE

It was perhaps the most extraordinary moment in the first 35 years of one-day cricket down-under. Michael Bevan spearheaded a remarkable revival, enabling Australia to defeat the West Indies by one wicket on New Year's Day, 1996, in Sydney. Bevan clubbed the very last ball of the match, from off-spinner Roger Harper, down the ground for four.

'It was one of those wonderful freakish occasions,' said coach Bob Simpson. 'Deep down you know that you should never win from there. It's one of the joys of one-day cricket, when it can produce something like that.'

Set 173 on a green seamer, the Australians collapsed early, needing 42 from the final six overs, and seven from the last. After Shane Warne was run out, No. 11 batsman Glenn McGrath stole a single, but Bevan couldn't score from the second-last delivery and four were still needed to win. Almost every West Indian fieldsman was sent into the outfield to protect the pickets.

Having nearly yorked himself the previous ball as he charged at Harper, Bevan again launched himself down the wicket. This time the ball was shorter, allowing him to swing his arms, and he timed it so sweetly that his shot evaded the boundary riders on either side and thudded over the far ropes.

'It was four from the moment I hit it,' Bevan said later, 'and I reckon my arms were in the air in triumph before the ball reached the boundary.'

The win ensured fresh notoriety for the quietly spoken New South Welshman. Soon he was to be the world's No. 1 one-day batsman.

SILKY SMOOTH

So silky smooth was Ted McDonald's run-up and action that he could have been bowling in carpet slippers. Even at 38, he was as fast as anyone in the world, and his noted partnership with Jack 'Gelignite' Gregory triggered unprecedented Australian success in the 1920s. The only one to compare with him was the West Indian Michael Holding, known as 'Whispering Death'.

SIMMO'S BIG BREAK

Multi-gifted Bobby Simpson was 16 and contemplating his first big decision in life. Having reduced his handicap to scratch at Marrickville G.C., he was seriously contemplating specialising in golf ahead of cricket when he received a phone call. Sid Barnes was unavailable for the New South Wales XI. Would he like to play?

'I'd put in my papers to be a [golf] apprentice, too,' said Simpson. 'There was a golf course just down the end of my street and every afternoon I was down there. I'd play with a few mates and some days we'd take it in turns to play a few holes left-handed. It was fun. Great times.

'But that phone call changed everything. It decided which way I was going. The decision was made for me. I loved golf and still do, but it didn't have the profile then that it does now.'

On debut against the visiting Victorians, Simpson made 44 not out and eight not out, including a six from the bowling of Ian Johnson, 'over cow corner'. He also remembers the verbals from Victoria's leg-spinner, Jack 'Snarler' Hill, who considered him a lucky young so-and-so to even be playing in such an august match, let alone making runs!

Now that he's almost 70, golf is again No. 1 for Simpson and he remains off single figures, at Concord.

SIXTY SECONDS OF INSANITY

It was one of those hot, sticky Melbourne days when even the sun-worshippers in Bay 13 were covering up. Seeing the strapping New Zealand All Black Brian McKechnie marching purposefully on to the ground with six to tie from just one ball, Australia's captain, Greg Chappell, panicked. The best-of-five World Series was all square at 1-1 and Chappell couldn't bear to contemplate having to win the competition via a fifth and deciding match. The Australian captain admits that everything got to him: the heat, the schedule, the pressure and, unlikely as it was, the prospect of McKechnie lobbing a ball into the stands.

Approaching his brother, Trevor, Greg said, 'How are you at bowling your underarms?' (Greg was referring back to the Chappell brothers' boyhood when, in their Adelaide backyard, Trevor – several years younger than Greg and Ian – could bowl nothing else.)

'Oh . . . I'm not sure. 'Aven't tried for a while.'

'Well, you're about to. Now.'

Addressing umpire Don Weser, Greg said, 'Don, Trevor is going to bowl the last ball underarm.'

'Pardon?'

'The last ball will be bowled underarm.'

'Hang on. I'll inform the batsman. And Peter [Cronin, the umpire at square leg].'

Trevor Chappell dutifully rolled the last ball along the ground, McKechnie blocked it and hurled his bat away in disgust. Australia may have won the cricket match but, in 60 seconds of insanity, its captain had brought disgrace upon himself and his team.

New Zealand's captain, Geoff Howarth, was livid and ran on to the ground, complaining to the umpires that underarm bowling had been outlawed. It had – but only in England. In the Victorian Cricket Association delegate's room, match referee Bob Parish was called to the telephone. It was long-distance: Adelaide. Even Sir Donald Bradman was incredulous.

As one of New Zealand's senior players furiously

threw a cup and saucer against the wall, and officials fumbled for a copy of the laws, there was an eerie silence in the Australian rooms – until the phone rang. Trevor Chappell was nearest. 'Greg Chappell? Not 'ere, mate. Wrong number.'

Sam Loxton, one of Bradman's Invincibles, came down the stairs with tears in his eyes. 'You may have won the game, son,' he said, addressing Chappell, 'but you've lost a lot of friends.' The only one with half a smile was Dennis Lillee. For once, someone else was in trouble. Fun-loving Dougie Walters attempted an ice-breaker. 'Well, they say that a cricket match is not over until the last ball is bowled!'

Chappell admits now that he was not fit to captain Australia that day. He was emotionally and physically spent.

Later, McKechnie said, 'Many people have forgotten that the best I could achieve was a tie. We couldn't actually win the game.'

SLASHER (I)

So superstitious was Queensland's much-loved all-rounder Ken 'Slasher' Mackay that he refused to have a chapter 13 in his autobiography, *Slasher Opens Up*.

SLASHER (II)

Before making the double-century in Sydney that clinched his first tour of England in 1956, Slasher Mackay rated his chances of a trip at two to one against. He said as much in the Sydney rooms and there was a rustling of paper as his Queensland teammates jumped on.

Never before had they cheered so enthusiastically, as Mackay made a career-transforming 203, after being dropped twice before he was 15.

SLEDGING WITH A SMILE

No one sledged as hard or as often as Les Favell. Long-time South Australian teammate Barry Jarman said Favell would abuse the bowlers while he was batting. Some were so taken aback they'd complain to the umpire.

'It was hilarious and he was good at it,' Jarman said. 'He used to tell them that they couldn't bowl, and then proceed to hook and cut them all over the Adelaide Oval.

'Terry Jenner was bowling against us one day, for Western Australia, and Les kept charging down the wicket to him, saying "Happy birthday!"

'Ian Chappell was at the other end and, on one occasion, went to call Les through for one. "You don't think you're getting down this end, son, do you?" Les said.'

On another occasion, on a belter in Adelaide, when first-time Victorian captain Jack Potter won the toss and told Les he could bat, the reply came quick as a flash, 'You won't get a hit!'

SEE: FAVOURITES FROM FAVELLI, PAGE 69

SO MUCH FOR BEING STODGY

From the time Justin Langer was struck six times before scoring his first run, on debut for Australia against the West Indies (Adelaide, 1992–93), he has been battling opinion. Langer says he was initially hurt by Kerry O'Keeffe's barb that he'd 'rather watch ripe bananas brown than watch Justin Langer bat'. But then he decided to use it as motivation.

In the study at his home in Perth, Langer has a favourite picture from a Test in Hobart, which shows a shot of the scoreboard: Hayden 1, Langer 50, Australia 0/55.

'So much for being stodgy!' he wrote in his book, *The Power and the Passion*.

SOBERS THE GREAT

It was the eve of the final game of 1963–64. South Australia had to win in Melbourne to take their first Sheffield Shield in more than a decade. The evening before the game, five of the leading South Australian players – Les Favell, Ian McLachlan, Barry Jarman, John Lill and Neil Hawke – invited themselves around to star all-rounder Garry Sobers' apartment.

There had been some negative comments made in a Melbourne newspaper by outspoken 'keeper Ray Jordon, and they wanted Sobers to know about it.

'You know that Slug Jordon reckons you can't bat and that you never make any runs against Victoria,' they said. 'We want you to show him . . .'

Sobers thanked them for coming and, over the next four days, made a century and took nine wickets as SA clinched the points it needed for the title.

'What do you think about Sobie now?' the South Australians said to Jordon at the after-match.

SPOTTING A SUPERSTAR

Cricket legend Doug Walters knew Glenn McGrath was a beauty.

'We were playing a Toohey's Cup match in Dubbo [in 1988] and he had me dropped first or second ball. It was clear he could bowl, but you had no idea he'd play 100 Tests or take almost 500 wickets,' he said.

Walters rang Steve Rixon, then involved at Sutherland, and recommended the club immediately select McGrath, then 18, in their first XI. Three years later, he was included in NSW's Sheffield Shield team and, soon afterwards, became the first Test player to be selected while still at the Commonwealth Bank Australian Cricket Academy.

Walters said it was his privilege to be back in England in 1997 to see McGrath devastate the home side with eight for 38 at Lord's.

'The pitch had a little bit in it and he was in devastating form,' Walters said.

STAN'S SPECIAL DAY

If any other bush cricketers have dominated a game quite like this, I'd like to hear about it. Representing Baxter against Pearcedale in the North Peninsula (now Mornington Peninsula) Cricket Association at Baxter in 1933–34, Stan Peters not only made 201 not out in a team score of 1/287 declared, he took seven for 61 and four for 14 as Pearcedale slipped to an innings defeat.

STAR APPRENTICES

Few have served a longer or more distinguished apprenticeship at first-class level than Victorian Brad Hodge who, in 2004, was co-opted into the Australian touring team to India, a prelude to his selection to New Zealand and England in 2005. While his actual game time on the subcontinent was limited to one inconsequential provincial match and 10 minutes as a substitute fielder (Nagpur, third Test), Hodge said it was still a career highlight to be part of the Australian squad that defeated India at home for the first time in 35 years. Having debuted as an 18-year-old, Hodge is one of a handful of Australians to make 10 000 first-class runs or more – and *not* play for Australia.

His mother, Val, says her son's love of ball-sports started as soon as he could walk.

MOST RUNS BEFORE THEIR FIRST TEST*

Martin Love
Queensland & Durham
Age at Test debut: 28
Seasons played: 11
Runs scored before first Test: 10 532

Darren Lehmann
South Australia & Victoria
Age: 27
Seasons: 11
Runs: 10 267

Mark Waugh
New South Wales & Essex
Age: 25
Seasons: 6
Runs: 7501

Greg Chappell
South Australia & Somerset
Age: 22
Seasons: 5
Runs: 5864

Stuart Law
Queensland
Age: 27
Seasons: 8
Runs: 5797

* statistics to the start of the 2005 English season

'He'd run around everywhere carrying a ball or a cut-down bat with him,' she said. 'He loved to hit the ball as high and as far as he could, and one of the gentlemen from school came over and asked if he could play in the local [Moorabbin] Under 12s cricket team, as he kept lobbing the ball over the fence at school.

'He and [another Victorian] Ian Hewitt would open the batting and the bowling in those days, and were always trying to outdo each other. I'd walk around the boundary saying, "Keep it down, Brad, keep it down." I didn't realise I must have sounded like a [broken] record.

'His coach, Graham Stewart, came up after the first game and told us we should have Brad coached. He reckoned he was a natural.'

Val said her son was also a budding baseballer with the Cheltenham Rustlers before, in his mid-teens, opting to specialise in cricket. The following year, he joined Premier League club Melbourne and debuted in the first XI, aged 16.

MOST RUNS BY AUSTRALIANS WITHOUT PLAYING A TEST

PLAYER	PERIOD	RUNS	100S	AVE
Ken Grieves	1945–46 to 1964	23 099	29	33.66
Bill Alley	1945–46 to 1968	19 612	31	31.88
Jamie Cox	1987–88 to 2004–05	18 554	51	43.14
Frank Tarrant	1898–99 to 1936–37	17 952	33	36.41
Brad Hodge	1993–94 to 2004–05	11 927	36	47.51

'I was always driving him around to games,' Val said. 'But I love it. I could sit and watch cricket each and every day and not miss a ball. John [Brad's father] is just as proud but he likes keeping himself busy, doing a spot of gardening or something like that. He can't watch like I can.'

A STAR IS BORN

Arthur Morris was a lower-order batsman and part-time spin bowler when Bill O'Reilly returned from Test duty to captain St George (1936–37). O'Reilly liked the teenager's style, particularly his hook shot, and immediately promoted him to opening.

'We were playing Central Cumberland, for whom Lou Benaud, Richie's father, was playing,' said O'Reilly. 'On winning the toss, I walked into the rooms and said, "Put 'em on, Artie".

'He made 60 or 70 in exquisite style and, when he got out, I congratulated him and got hold of his bat. It was a gnarled old thing, discoloured from too much oil, and had all this sticking plaster holding it together.

'"You're not going to use this bat anymore," I said to him.

'"But I like this bat . . ."

'"I'll get you another."'

O'Reilly was as good as his word, ordering a new bat from Stan McCabe's sports store. Two years later, at 18, Morris became the first player ever to score twin centuries on his first-class debut. A star was born.

A STAR-TO-BE

Few batsmen, even at junior level, have so dominated a century stand. Falconer Street State School (North Fitzroy) was playing Moonee Ponds in a schoolboys' final at the Fitzroy Cricket Ground in the early forties. The openers, budding Test champion Neil Harvey and football umpire-to-be Harry Beitzel, started with a century for the first wicket. Beitzel's contribution? Two.

STOOL PIGEON

Inadvertently, Leo O'Brien always insisted, he was the stool pigeon in publicising Bill Woodfull's famous Bodyline quote: 'There are two teams out there and only one is playing cricket.' O'Brien was twelfth man in the Adelaide Test of 1932–33 and was in the rooms when Woodfull emerged from the showers, sporting a huge welt above the heart where he'd been struck by the Nottinghamshire expressman, Harold Larwood.

'Are you all right, Bill?' O'Brien asked.

'It's not good out there, Leo. It's not good.'

As Woodfull was dressing, there was a knock on the Australian dressing-room door, and P.F. 'Plum' Warner and Richard Palairet (the two MCC managers) walked in to pay their respects. Woodfull said he didn't want to see them and told them England was playing in an unsporting fashion. 'Gentlemen,' he said, 'that's all I have to say.'

'There were only five of us in the room at the time,' said O'Brien. 'Me, the men from MCC, Woody and our masseur – who was deaf, so it couldn't have been him! I went back outside and told the boys what had happened. Within 24 hours, it was in the [Sydney] papers. One of our own players must have spilt the beans, but I don't know who.'

It was during the same game that O'Brien, as a substitute fieldsman, caught Herbert Sutcliffe with an Australian Rules-style catch high above his head, as he ran around the fine-leg boundary. Like the others, O'Brien hated Bodyline and said the 61 he made in the final Test in Sydney was just about the best knock of his life. He was thrilled, too, to tour South Africa in 1935–36. Several of his treasured happy snaps are included in this book.

STRATFORD'S FINEST SON

At 73, Bill Young says he's in retirement mode. But he still insists on riding his bike and joining wife, Lynne, for a six-kilometre run most days. One of Gippsland's most celebrated sportsmen, Young was good enough to top-score with 56 against Len Hutton's 1954–55 touring MCC team at Yallourn, as well as head the VFL goal-kicking in his very first year with St Kilda Football Club. On several occasions, he played with St Kilda Cricket Club in the district cricket grand final and, the following Saturday, lined up at full-forward in round 1 with the footballing Saints.

'As soon as one season finished, I'd be into the other,' said multi-gifted Bill, who is a legend in and around Sale and Stratford.

STREETS AHEAD

One of the high points of my very modest cricket career came one day at the MCG, when I found myself under a skyer from cricket-loving Prime Minister Bob Hawke.

'First time I've been caught out by a journalist for 25 years,' quipped the PM, ever so sharp even on his day off.

The bowler was Tony Street, the elfin former cabinet minister from the days of the Fraser Government.

'I can't remember *not* getting Bob out in any of those [friendly] games,' said Street. 'He was forever trying to hit me for six.'

While his public duties took precedence over his sporting career, Street, pre-politics, was an outstanding leg-spinner, good enough to play against two South African touring teams.

The Street family farm was at Lismore, 20 km north of Camperdown. Tony's father, Geoffrey, was a former Melbourne Cricket Club teammate of Australian legends Warwick Armstrong and Vernon Ransford.

'Dad [also a politician] bowled leg-breaks like me, but was probably faster through the air,' said Street. 'He had an extraordinary, unpickable wrong 'un. He'd been shot through the wrist [during World War I] and could only bend it so much.

'Playing cricket was second nature to me. I'd carry an old tennis ball around in my pocket, constantly squeezing it to strengthen my fingers. After work [on the farm], I'd get out a hanky and put it on a good length, positioning it either for a right-hander or a left-hander [batsman], and bowl an eight-ball over before foxing all the balls again. I'd do it for hours.'

Street was in Melbourne Grammar's first XI as a 15-year-old, and was a regular at Country Week before going into the navy. His career-best 16-wicket haul (seven for 49 and nine for 11) came all in one day on a dry, bouncy Eastern Oval in Ballarat, and ensured the Western Plains an outright victory.

Like the best leg-spinners, Street had two googlies – one easy to spot and one tougher to pick.

'I'd bowl the easier one to a batsman early on and, if he couldn't pick it, I wouldn't bother to bowl the second one, as it was harder to bowl. I'd keep it in reserve against somebody I reckoned could play.'

Street says he was almost part of history at the MCG one day just after the War when Percy Beames, recently retired from first-class cricket, lofted an on-drive on to the balcony of the old MCC members' stand.

'It soared straight at the clock and only needed another yard or two and it would have struck it. It was a huge hit.

I've never heard of anybody getting so close to the clock as Percy did that day.'

Of the best country players he opposed, Street named Henry Gunstone from the Grampians, Stewart Austin from the Western Plains, Warrnambool's Ian 'Lefty' Wright and Horsham's Kevin Officer as among the very best. And the best cricketing politician, according to Street, was Sam Calder. Known as 'Not-so-silent Sam', Calder was the member for the Northern Territory, a former opening bat for Melbourne and one of the Top End's all-time finest sportsmen.

A STUNNING SELECTION

Ian Meckiff's no-balling for throwing in the opening Test in Brisbane (December, 1963) may have been pre-meditated, and designed to stamp throwers out of world cricket once and for all, according to the leader of South Africa's pace attack, Peter Pollock. Pollock said Meckiff's selection was a shot from left field, triggered by South Africa's defeat of powerful New South Wales by an innings on the eve of the internationals.

'Even the Australian selectors, under the leadership of Sir Donald Bradman, appeared to panic,' he said in his autobiography, *God's Own Fast Bowler*.

'The loss to retirement of famous left-arm speedster Alan Davidson rattled them into including controversial Ian Meckiff. We were stunned by his inclusion.

'Bradman was known to oppose Meckiff's action and inclusion, so it was assumed that he was outvoted. Others suggested that Bradman, sick and tired of continually being pestered by parochial Victorian fans, wanted him tested and put out of the game once and for all. Maybe the real truth lay somewhere in between.'

SEE: LIFETIME SCARS, PAGE 119

SUBTLE AS A SLEDGEHAMMER

The sun was setting late one afternoon in Sydney and umpire Dick French crossed over to point for a clearer view. Passing Ian Chappell, whom he'd never met before, French said, 'Just going to point, Ian.'

'I don't give a f— where you stand,' came the reply. And then, 'While you're at it, you can tell your equally incompetent mate that he's not watching the no-balls!'

French insists it's true.

A SURE THING

Batting with only 10 men is commonplace in less serious cricket circles – but definitely not in the old-time 'Wars of the Roses' matches between Victoria and New South Wales, which were played each Christmas from the 1890s to the 1960s. (After this, they were replaced by the Boxing Day Test.)

It was Boxing Day, 1931, and four of the Victorians – bosom buddies Leo O'Brien, Len Darling, Bill Ponsford and Harry 'Bull' Alexander – had been given a tip for the first race at Caulfield. They went into the MCC members' bar to give some money to a barman friend who'd offered to place their bets. But he wasn't going to the track until after lunch. Pity to pass on a 'sure thing', the boys reckoned. So Alexander, the last man in, took a cable tram to Flinders Street Railway Station and then a train out to the racetrack, another 20 minutes away. With players like Ponsford (not out overnight), Keith Rigg and Jack Ryder to bat, it seemed inconceivable that Alexander would be needed until late in the afternoon. Teammate Jack Ellis often left a game to inspect nearby roadworks.

On his way back to the ground, the Bull found the tram so crowded that he could hardly get a foot in. Later, he told cricket writer Ray Robinson that he heard the gripman say that the 10-man Victorians were out cheaply and NSW was batting a second time.

'Harry pulled his hat down, so as not to be recognised as the missing last man,' said Robinson. 'At the ground, he found that leg-spinner Bill O'Reilly had taken five for 22 on his Melbourne debut, and the only double-figure scorers had been his mates, O'Brien and Darling.

'At the luncheon interval, [captain Bill] Woodfull called, "Come here, Harry" and, admonishing him, said he was risking his place in the team.

'Executive Chairman Dr Reg Morton wound up a much more severe rebuke with, "You must *never* leave the ground, Alexander, even if you are a rabbit."

'Harry assured him he would never be at fault again, "although I'm only a ferret and go in after the rabbits".'

And the 'sure thing'? It was beaten.

SWEET REVENGE

Standing on the balcony at Old Trafford after Australia had retained the Ashes in 1961, rookie opener Bill Lawry saw the emotion of old campaigners Neil Harvey, Richie Benaud and Ken 'Slasher' Mackay. They had all been part of Australia's previous, unsuccessful campaign in '56. Until then, Lawry hadn't truly realised how satisfying it was to defeat England and how much it meant to so many.

'You could just see it in their faces,' he said. 'Someone like Neil Harvey, for example, had made centuries under Bradman, but he also made a pair against Jim Laker at the same ground in '56 . He was a truly great player. And I'll never forget his 167 against Laker and [Tony] Lock in the 1958–59 Melbourne Test. He just didn't allow them to hit the wicket, so quick was his footwork. It must have been sweet revenge.'

t

|||||||||||

TAKING A CHANCE (I)

It had been raining for days in Sydney and Ray 'Slug' Jordon, Victoria's colourful wicketkeeper, reckoned there was no way the game could possibly start as scheduled. It was hot and he had a thirst, so he went for it.

Much to his dismay, it was fine and sunny on match morning, and the covers had kept the rain off the ground. His sore head became even sorer when he was told that captain Bill Lawry had 'dobbed' them. Jordon did his best to buckle his pads and out he went, conceding byes from the first two Ian Meckiff deliveries. On the third, his instincts took over and he grabbed an ever-so-fine tickle, diving full-stretch to his left.

'You beauty,' he said. 'That's the first time I've taken a catch off the first ball of a match!'

TAKING A CHANCE (II)

It was one of the most action-packed opening overs ever: Bob Simpson 18 and Australia 0/18 after just eight balls from the West Indian expressman, Wes Hall.

'We'd had a great contest the whole way through in that series,' said Simpson. 'It was my first series as opening batsman and Wes was very, very quick. It was the last Test and he was getting tired. I was lucky enough in the second innings to take 18 runs from his first over and another nine off his second. It was about the only time I felt it was a pretty good job being out there.

'I'd taken 16 off him in the first over in an Australian XI game in Hobart not long before. On this occasion, he just happened to bowl the ball in spots I thought I could hit.'

Simpson's opening partner, Colin McDonald, had the best seat in the house from the opposite end, and had a slightly different slant on the MCG onslaught.

'Wes was lightning-quick that day,' he said, 'and Bobby was shit-scared. He was backing away and knocking the ball over the top. They were audacious shots.'

Audacious or not, Simpson's 92 was top score as Australia clinched the deciding Test by just two wickets. Hall was a victim of Simpson's opening salvo with none for 40 from just five overs.

TALL TALES AND TRUE (I)

One of the few ever responsible for picking *both* teams in a first-class match was Bill Jacobs in the 1971–72 summer, when he was appointed manager of the Rest of the World team in Australia. At the time, Jacobs was a Victorian selector and, in tandem with ROW captain Garry Sobers, also picked the World XIs during their memorable Australia-wide tour, highlighted by Sobers' epic 254 in Melbourne.

TALL TALES AND TRUE (II)

Victor Troffitt was a fine club cricketer at Geelong. One day he came home, flopped into his easy chair and told his wife, 'Well darling, I've finally done it.'

'Done what, darling?'

'100 wickets and 1000 runs.'

'My dear,' she said, 'you must be exhausted. I'll make you a cup of tea!'

TALL TALES AND TRUE (III)

Ernie McCormick was known as 'Fast and Funny' to his mates, a great joker and the life of every party. Strappingly tall and, on his best days, furiously fast, he was good enough to tour South Africa and England. As a batsman, however, he was truly in the bunny class. When asked where he used to bat, he'd invariably say, 'Just before the roller'.

During his England visit (1938), McCormick aggregated less than 50 runs, despite using a bat Don Bradman had given him. On returning to Melbourne, he remembered a promise he'd made to a young hero-worshipper and handed it over.

'But I never expected a new one!' said the delighted child. There wasn't a mark on it.

TANGLING WITH TRUEMAN

Umpire Bill Smyth asked a favour as he was walking out with Col Egar to stand in his first Test match (Melbourne, 1962–63).

'I'd like to take the opener,' he said.

'Why?' asked Egar.

'I want to get the agony over and done with!'

'It was something I never thought would come my way,' said Smyth. 'Freddie Trueman was bowling and Bill Lawry was on strike, and he hit Bill on the pads outside the leg stump. I stood there and, with a smile on my face, said, "Not out". As Fred walked back past me, he muttered, "Just wanted to see if you were fooking awake!" I felt good after that.'

TARGET GODDARD

Tom Goddard, Gloucestershire's 47-year-old spin-wizard, was being touted as a likely reinforcement for England's team when the 1948 Australians arrived at Bristol. They promptly made 7/774 declared, with Arthur Morris motoring to a career-best 290. Morris made a hundred before lunch and a hundred before tea. He was on the brink of a third century before stumps, when he hit a full toss back to the bowler.

Morris had made a point of targeting Goddard, jumping cat-like down the wicket to drive, and thumping any short ones through midwicket. With figures of none for 186, Goddard was never spoken of again as a potential Ashes bowler – despite taking 122 county wickets that season at a strike-rate of almost five a game.

TEST-MATCH TERRY

The '89 Australians have never let Terry Alderman forget that he played more Tests than county games during his superlative Ashes summer in England. When some of the players played as many as 17 or 18 first-class games, Alderman played only 11, including six Tests and just five of the less frenetic county fixtures. Many of his mates still delight in calling him 'Test-match Terry'.

THANKS, JOHNNO

But for the benevolence of Melburnian Ian Johnson, John J. Warr of Cambridge University, Middlesex and England would not have the worst-ever Ashes bowling average (281) today. Selected only twice for England, in Sydney and Adelaide during the MCC's 1950–51 tour, Warr returned match figures of none for 142 on debut, before taking none for 63 in the first innings of the fourth Test. His figures further deteriorated in the second innings until Johnson, Australia's captain-to-be, tickled one behind.

'It was so slight John could never have heard it,' said Johnson. 'It was barely a feather. The wicketkeeper,

Godfrey Evans, inquired. Warr followed, roaring his support at the possibility of finally taking a wicket. Umpire Cocks, however, was unmoved and Warr's face fell when he thought he'd missed out again.

'Normally I never walked, but I saw his disappointment, nodded to the umpire and walked off. It was the only time in a Test I ever did that.'

'THESE AUSTRALIANS ARE UP TO SOMETHING'

The Old Trafford Test of 1921 will always be remembered as the game in which Australia's maverick captain, Warwick Armstrong, sent down two successive overs after a delay in play. Unlike in Australia, where timeless Tests were played, Tests that English summer were of three days' duration. After the opening day's play was lost through rain at Old Trafford, the game was played under two-day conditions.

'England batted on a wet wicket – not a sticky, but one which favoured batsmen, because the ball became wet and soggy and difficult to control,' said Australian Hunter 'Stork' Hendry, reminiscing about the tour.

'[C. A. G.] Russell was batting very well and we were in a very precarious position. Lots of runs were on the board and the possibility of a sticky faced us when it was our turn to occupy the crease. Sammy Carter, who was an encyclopaedia on cricket laws, said to Warwick, "If they don't close before 10 to five, they can't close today," and left the rule book open on his locker on the correct page before we took the field after the tea adjournment.

'Play went on and we were anxiously watching the clock, and heaved sighs of relief when 5 p.m. came.

'The Hon. Lionel Tennyson [England's captain] came on to the dressing-room balcony almost immediately and very jubilantly called out that he had closed their innings.

(In his book, *Sticky Wickets*, he claimed the time to be 5.50 p.m., with 30 minutes still to play.) Warwick made several attempts to show him we were not going off, but Lionel had disappeared into the dressing-room. There was nothing else for us to do but to go off.

'Warwick then produced the rule book after everyone, including selectors and administrators, disputed the decision. It was an unusual occasion to point out that they did not know their own rules!

'The Sydney Hill was noted in those days for barracking, but I never heard worse than when we trooped back on to the field [after a 15-minute hiatus]. Even when passing through the members' enclosure, we were abused and bustled. Bedlam broke out all around the ground. So Warwick sat down on the wicket, just like a bull elephant, and waited until Tennyson came on to the ground, and walked around the whole arena with an umpire, explaining it was their fault and not the Australians' [fault].

'Play was then resumed and Warwick, who had bowled the last over before we left the field, picked up the ball and bowled another – this time from the opposite end! Only Warwick could have done that.'

Earlier, watching from the grandstand, ex-England captain Archie Maclaren had commented, 'These Australians are up to something,' as they kept looking at the ground clock.

THEY HAD TO BRUSH THEIR TEETH WITH FOSTER'S

Rather than staying in plush international hotels on the subcontinent, Australian teams of the not-so-distant past had to contend with less comfortable sleeping arrangements, and eating and drinking the bare minimum for fear of falling ill. So stricken was the team on the 1959–60 tour that manager Sam Loxton had to fill in for one match!

'In a place called the Ritz in Ahmedabad,' said Colin McDonald, 'you couldn't drink the water, so we brushed our teeth in Foster's Lager.'

Several of the touring team, most notably Gavin Stevens and Gordon Rorke, caught hepatitis and never represented Australia again.

THEY SAID IT

Dennis Lillee (1982): *There are times when I'd like to disappear off the face of the earth, or wear a mask that no one would ever recognise me in.*

Kerry O'Keeffe (2004): *He [Michael Clarke] has got such a youthful face . . . he'll be producing his driver's licence in nightclubs when he's 35!*

THOMMO

Loping in from just 10–12 metres before slinging the ball at speeds close to 160 km/h (100 mph), Jeff Thomson took three for 59 and six for 46 on his unforgettable Ashes debut, as Australia completed a first-Test victory in four days and 80 minutes (Brisbane, 1974–5).

Two key Englishmen, Dennis Amiss and John Edrich, suffered hand fractures off Thomson's bowling on one of the bounciest 'Gabba wickets in years, prepared in the final week by Brisbane's jack-of-all-trades Lord Mayor, Clem Jones.

'You can throw in all the fastest of the West Indians, [but] Thommo was quicker than them all by two yards,' said Greg Chappell, who was later the best man at Thommo's wedding.

THREE IN THREE

It was the most convoluted, confusing hat-trick in Test history – the days Merv Hughes took three wickets in three balls from three different overs, against the West Indies at the WACA Ground (Perth, 1988–89). After having Curtly Ambrose caught behind with the sixth ball of his thirty-seventh over, Hughes ended the West Indian first innings with the first of his thirty-eighth, when No. 11 Patrick Patterson fell to a catch by Hughes's Footscray teammate, Tony Dodemaide.

A day and a half later, taking the new ball at the start of the West Indian second innings, Hughes dismissed Gordon Greenidge lbw with his first delivery. At the time, few realised it was a hat-trick. Hughes was only alerted to the fact by the boundary-riding Steve Waugh, who had heard it over the radio.

As Hughes was lacing up his boots, half an hour before the opening of the second innings, coach Bobby Simpson had asked how he intended to attack it.

'Bounce the hell out of 'em,' said Hughes, looking for some retribution after Geoff Lawson had suffered a broken jaw.

'No Merv,' Simpson had said. 'Bowl line and length. Bowl on the stumps. We might get a couple of them out before the close. That'll put 'em on the back foot.'

'Allan Border was next,' said Hughes. Border thought Hughes looked like a caveman and liked to call him 'Grump'.

'Grump,' Border instructed, 'bowl in the corridor of uncertainty.'

'To this day I don't know what he meant,' remembers Hughes. 'But I made sure the first one was up there. He [Greenidge] missed it and we got the lb.'

TIME OF THE TYPHOON

No wonder they called Frank Tyson 'Typhoon'. His onslaught against the Australians at Northants in 1953 was the quickest of the Coronation tour.

'Lindsay Hassett had the match off and Arthur Morris was captain,' recalled Neil Harvey. 'We were sent in and I was still in my civvies as I watched the opening over. Tyson had Colin McDonald lbw second ball. I asked Graeme Hole if he'd mind going in at three. Two balls later, he was out, and I still wasn't ready. So Jimmy de Courcy went in. He lasted the over, only to fall at the other end. When I got out there, we were 3/10 and Artie said to me, "Where the bloody hell have you been?"'

The pair added 175 – Harvey scored a century, Morris 80 – and the Australians won by an innings inside two days.

TIPS OF THE TRADE

During his first tour of England in 1953, a young Richie Benaud asked legendary Bill O'Reilly if there were any tips he could give him.

'Yes,' said the Tiger, covering the tour as a journalist. 'Learn to bowl a big leg-break and pitch it on a length every time. But be patient. It'll take you four years to be able to do it.'

By 1957, Benaud was the outstanding wrist-spinner in the world and was to finish, seven years later, with a then-record 248 Test wickets.

In 1990, Benaud was a guest at a Victorian Cricket Association golf day at Royal Melbourne, and was asked by a young Shane Warne if there was a tip or two he'd like to pass on. Benaud duly told him about Bill O'Reilly's advice, and emphasised that it would take the young Victorian years to truly control the leg-break.

'Unlike me, though, he took just two years, not four – phenomenal! If I had my time over again, I'd bowl more like Warne than I did Benaud,' the old champion said.

TOLD YOU

Having taken a wicket with the fifth ball of his Test debut, at Rawalpindi (1998–99), Colin Miller took 30 overs to get another.

'I was bowling off-spin from around the wicket and reckoned I must have appealed for lb 16 or 17 times, none of which were given,' Miller said.

'Finally, [umpire] Peter Willey turned to me and said, "Look, I bowled off-spin professionally for 20 years and can't remember once getting an lbw from around the wicket. Go over."

'I did and, to my very next appeal [against the left-handed Saeed Anwar], Willey raised his finger. "Told you," he said.'

TOP THAT

Change bowler Keith Stackpole can picture each one of his 15 Test wickets. It's inconsequential that more than half his victims had already made centuries, including Graeme Pollock (274) and Denis Lindsay (182).

'They are all in *Wisden*,' he says, smiling in the knowledge that no one can take his wickets away. 'Pollock was out caught and bowled, but I was lucky to get Denis Lindsay. He'd already hit five sixes and this one was going over, too, but for Ian Chappell pocketing a magnificent catch at deep square, right on the fence, at Jo'burg.'

TOP TWELVE INNINGS

The opposition were mediocre, but Matthew Hayden's colossal 380 against Zimbabwe in Perth in 2003–04 was a triumph of skill, strokeplay and fitness. It truly deserves to rate alongside the most acclaimed innings by Australians in Test history. My top 12 of all time are:

1. **Don Bradman, 334 v. England, Leeds, 1930**
   The Don was the first to make 300 runs in a day's play.
2. **Stan McCabe, 187 v. England, Sydney, 1932–33**
   The bravest knock ever, which almost buried Bodyline just as it was starting.
3. **Allan Border, 100 not out v. West Indies, Port of Spain, 1983–84**
   His finest hour against the most lethal attack in history.
4. **Don Bradman, 270 v. England, Melbourne, 1936–37**
   At 2-0 down after the first two Tests, Australia was down and almost out.
5. **Mark Waugh, 116 v. South Africa, Port Elizabeth, 1996–97**
   A match-winning knock on a green wicket in a world-title bout.
6. **Neil Harvey, 151 v. South Africa, Durban, 1949–50**
   A miraculous knock against quality bowling and on a wicket turning square.
7. **Steve Waugh, 200 v. West Indies, Kingston, 1995**
   Enabled Australia to wrest the World Championship after 15 years of West Indian domination.
8. **Dean Jones, 210 v. India, Madras, 1986–87**
   Made in searing heat and in an epic game that ended in a tie.
9. **Matthew Hayden, 380 v. Zimbabwe, Perth, 2003–04**
   The highest Test innings by an Australian, a monumental feat of focus and strokeplay.

10. **Peter Burge, 160 v. England, Leeds, 1964**
    One of the greatest against-the-odds Ashes innings.
11. **Clem Hill, 188 v. England, Melbourne, 1897–98**
    Including 182 runs in a day, the most ever in an MCG Test, bar Bradman and India's Virender Sehwag.
12. **Kim Hughes, 100 not out v. West Indies, Melbourne, 1981–82**
    An incredibly brave innings after Australia was 4/26 and crumbling against the best attack in the world.

TOUGH AS TEAK

Behind Ian Redpath's ready smile and amiable manner was one tough cricketer. Thumped on the chest one day by Andy Roberts's change-up bouncer, Redpath returned Roberts's icy stare and batted on. So hard a blow was it, however, that Redpath couldn't walk the following day. To protect his chest the next time they played, he had a pocket stitched into his cricket shirt into which he inserted a thigh pad.

'I didn't want to take another one like that,' he said.

TOURING TEAMS – THE WORST EVER

Until Nasser Hussain's much-maligned Englishmen won the final Test in Sydney in 2002–03, his team was the worst-performed ever to visit Australian shores. They won only twice in their first 10 weeks and, with Graham Thorpe electing not to come, Darren Gough breaking down before he'd bowled even one ball, and 'Aussie Alec' Stewart past his best, the Englishmen were outplayed from the start. Only opening batsman Michael Vaughan was of genuine world-class standard.

Previously, the worst-performed touring team was Sri Lanka, which won only six of almost 30 games in 1989–90. Their low point came on Christmas Eve, when they were defeated by a bunch of Saturday-afternoon malthoid cricketers representing the Victorian Country League, at Hastings. It was the first time in more than 90 years that a touring team had been beaten by a country side. The Mornington Peninsula's Bradman of the bush, Robert Bedford, topped off the day by twice lofting a young Sanath Jayasuriya over the huge pine trees and into the adjoining hayfields at midwicket.

Mohammad Azharuddin's 1991–92 Indians were almost as inept. From the time Azharuddin strained a groin while picking up a suitcase on arrival at Perth airport, the Indians lurched from disaster to disaster. Not even the emergence of teenage star Sachin Tendulkar could hide their deficiencies. Until Azhar scored a breathtaking 106 in his final innings of the tour, in Adelaide, he was averaging 16 in internationals – equal to the most unsuccessful batting captain to Australia, England's Mike Brearley.

The most embarrassing weekend a touring team has ever endured came in 1994–95, when Mike Atherton's injury-hit Englishmen lost twice to the kids of the Australian Cricket Academy, in between the first and second Tests. Budding international Ian Harvey's 80 from 89 balls clinched the shock first-up win, while fellow Victorian Brad Hodge's 96 not out was a match-winner the following day.

Asked for the reaction from the dressing-rooms, English tour manager Keith Fletcher said, 'There is a deathly hush in there. They are all sitting there feeling ashamed and, as an international side, so they should.'

Six additions were made to the 16-man touring party during England's nightmarish visit, with five injured players flying home at various stages. Another original tour-squad member, fast bowler Joey Benjamin, suffered a bout of chicken pox and was in quarantine for weeks.

THE WORST-EVER TOURING TEAMS

Team/season	Mts	Won	Lost	Drawn	Tied	Win %
Sri Lanka, 1989–90	29	6	15	8	-	20
West Indies, 2000–01	22	5	15	2	-	22
New Zealand, 1997–98	21	5	13	2	1	23
India, 1991–92	21	5	14	1	1	23
England, 2002–03	24	4	15	5	-	25
India, 1967–68	15	4	6	5	-	26
England, 1990–91	28	8	14	6	-	27

TRULY HERCULEAN

When it comes to performing above and beyond the call of duty, Tom Veivers' record of bowling 90 overs in an innings is truly Herculean. The ever-smiling Queenslander ripped the skin off his spinning finger during his marathon stint at Old Trafford in 1964, when he all but cracked West Indian Sonny Ramadhin's Test record of 95 overs.

'I bowled all day from the one end, apart from the last 20 minutes, when England eventually got out. John Price took a big swing at a full toss from me and was bowled, much to the disappointment of everyone – me, the Australian players, the England players and the crowd, who were all waiting for me to break the world record,' said Veivers.

'It was cool and a huge wind was blowing, making it hard for fast bowlers. Simmo [Bob Simpson] said, "I think you'd better bowl the first over today." First ball, Ken Barrington edged between the 'keeper, Wally Grout, and Simmo at slip. It was about the only half-chance he gave all day.

'Simmo came up and told me to continue. And that was it. He kept me going.'

This was the epic Test in which Simpson made 311 and Barrington 256. Veivers finished with three for 155 in the one-sided batting feast – just 18 wickets fell in five days.

u

UNDERSTUDIES

Brett Lee created a record, of sorts, when named twelfth man for the sixth Test in a row (Melbourne, 2004–05). (Queenslander Andy Bichel was Australia's twelfth man a record 19 times.) Lee was permanent drinks waiter from Nagpur in late October to Melbourne in December (2004), and again in New Zealand for three consecutive Tests in March (2005).

Previously, Ken Archer was an understudy throughout the entire 1949–50 tour of South Africa (five Tests). And he found himself twelfth man again for the first Ashes Test the following Australian summer. A top-order specialist, Archer says Australia's first six players were all champions and he found it impossible to break in.

'When Siddy Barnes retired, there was a possibility, so I opened a few times with Queensland and fluked a few games [for Australia], opening up with Arthur Morris – not that we did any good, mind you!'

Asked about his permanent understudy role in South Africa, Archer said, 'When the team first went over there, I thought I was a possibility and so did [South Australian fast bowler] Geff Noblet. We decided that one of us would get a game, depending on balance. When Bill Johnston got hurt, however, they flew [Keith] Miller over, and that was it for both of us (though Geff did play in the last one, replacing Ray Lindwall, of all people).'

As twelfth man, Archer said his duties ranged from collecting autograph sheets to stocking the fridge.

'I did get to go out onto the field in three or four of the Tests. Didn't take a catch . . . but I was out there on the paddock for a couple of hours, anyway.'

Archer says the Australian teams of the late forties and early fifties were as invincible as the teams of today.

'In the end, the Australian crowd used to barrack against us,' he said. 'They wanted more of a contest.'

UNFORGETTABLE MOMENTS (I)

Ask Sam Loxton about his major memory of the unforgettable 1948 tour and he settles on the moment Neil Harvey made a century on his Ashes debut in the epic fourth Test at Leeds.

'Keith Miller had just got out,' said Loxton, 'and Neil met me as I walked in. "We're right, Slox . . . They can't bowl!"'

'He [Harvey] was a cheeky little 19-year-old. He made 112. It was the thrill of the tour as far as I was concerned. We shared a room, cabins, trains, everything else. Lindsay Hassett, way back in 1947 on the Spencer Street Railway Station, made me responsible for looking after him. I'm more or less a father to him.'

Earlier in the tour, Harvey had asked Loxton to approach team captain Don Bradman on his behalf, to ask if he had a tip to help him make some runs.

'English conditions were so different to Australian ones,' said Harvey. 'I was having trouble and averaging seven after three games. I was starting to worry.'

So Loxton went to Bradman, whom he always called 'George', and said, 'George my young mate has got a problem. He's not making runs. Can you tell him what he's doing wrong?'

'Sammy,' said Bradman, 'go and tell your little mate if you keep the ball on the ground, you can't get out!'

Harvey was to make more than 1000 runs at an average of more than 50 for the tour, in which Australia remained unbeaten in all 34 games.

UNFORGETTABLE MOMENTS (II)

Not everyone has the opportunity to oppose a Bradman, a Sobers or a Viv Richards. Even fewer can say they actually dismissed them. So chuffed was the old Somerset bowler Bill Andrews when he bowled Bradman during Australia's 1938 tour that he entitled his autobiography *The Hand that Bowled Bradman*. In smaller print was the Don's score: 202!

Left-arm spin bowler Murray Bennett, from Bradman's old club St George, enjoyed his 15 minutes of fame in the New Year Test of 1985. He bowled the formidable Richards with his 'arm' ball, the highlight of his 11 Australian appearances.

'Viv had made 208 the Test before, and I copped a thumping [none for 78 from 20 overs on debut],' Bennett said. 'It was nice in the next Test [in Sydney, where he was based] to get a wicket more conducive to spin bowling, and I was able to support Bobby Holland, who bowled superbly. The odd one of mine was drifting back in, and three or four overs earlier he'd only just chopped one out which had come back with the arm. I thought there may be an opening but, against a batsman of that ability, you're never in control. It's more *hoping* that something like that will work.

'He went for the cut shot again, was cramped for room and was bowled. It was very sweet, especially as we beat them for the only time all summer.'

Bennett took five wickets for the match and Holland took 10.

UP THERE, ABLEY!

With 12 first-XI premierships and 400-odd games of cricket, Gary Abley is rightly ranked as Violet Town's finest cricketing son. Hoping one day to play alongside his teenage son, Nick, 41-year-old Abley says sport and family go hand-in-hand in the bush.

'It's just something you do,' he says.

He played four years in the big smoke with North Melbourne, as a teenager, before returning to Violet Town and becoming captain at the age of 18. He says a grand final win against Wanderers was one of the great all-time games of bush cricket.

'It went into a fourth day and we were still batting 100 runs behind. They got the final wickets and grabbed a lead of about 70, only for us to roll them for 40 or 50 and make the runs. We absolutely pinched it. It was extraordinary. We gave a kid [Mitch Cullen] who had hardly bowled all year a bowl, and he took five for 1! All their supporters had come and thought we were beaten. We did, too!'

UPSTAGED

Don Bradman a Victorian? It almost happened. After the death of Hugh Trumble, one of the giants of Australian cricket, in 1938, the Don was persuaded to apply for Trumble's job as secretary of the Melbourne Cricket Club.

'A great friend of mine in Melbourne reckoned it was the greatest job in Australian sport and I only had to put in an application and the job would be mine,' Bradman said. 'I thought he must have known what he was talking about, so I put in an application, only for Vernie [ex-Testman Vernon Ransford] to get the job on, as I understand it, the casting vote of the president.'

V

|||||||||||

'V' FOR VICTORY

Other than once opening Australia's bowling, alongside expressman Jeff Thomson, Trevor 'Larry' Laughlin's proudest moment in cricket was Victoria's mighty comeback to snatch the Sheffield Shield from Ian Chappell's South Australians in 1979–80.

'South Australia had batted themselves into a winning position, but we just never gave up and, in the end Higgsy [Jim Higgs] spun 'em out,' said Laughlin. 'They had the Shield in the official luncheon room and Dick Telford [Victoria's coach] had to give a speech at lunch. At 1/90 [chasing 244], everyone else in the room thought the Sackers were going to waltz in.

'But in the first over [after lunch], we got Ian Chappell out [for 32], and Dick looked around and said, "You've got another half an hour to look at the trophy . . . because it's going back to Victoria." And that's what happened.

'Dick not only coached us to back-to-back Shield wins; we won the 'Hamburger' [McDonald's] Cup under him as well.'

With 73 not out and 51 in what was virtually a final, Laughlin was one of the linchpins in Victoria's back-to-back titles, the first for 45 years.

THE VALOUR AWARD

When Cricket Victoria held its annual media and sponsor's recognition luncheon (May, 2004), several grassroots legends, including Ararat's Bradman of the bush, Henry Gunstone (129 career centuries, including one on his wedding day), were honoured for their passion and commitment to the game.

A lesser-known guest of honour was Seabrook Cricket Club's Peter Civitella, 43. He won the Williamstown and District's A-grade bowling average, despite being born with a deformed right arm. A cricketer for 23 years with a career-best performance of eight for 18 to his credit, Civitella took more than 30 wickets with his left-arm mediums.

'I like to hide the ball behind my back at the start of a game,' Civitella says, 'and often the umpire will say, "Right-arm over?" I then show 'em my [deformed] arm and say, "Naw, probably not today, mate!"'

Civitella also proved to be a stubborn No. 11. In one match in 2003–04, he helped Seabrook to an unlikely one-wicket victory. Together, he and teammate Bruno Raunik added 57 for the last wicket (Civitella's share was six). 'I love cricket, always have, always will,' he said.

W

||||||||||||

WAGGA WAGGA RICHES

Wagga Wagga, Australia's largest inland city, has produced four Test cricketers in the last 25 years: Steve Rixon, Geoff Lawson, Mark Taylor (who was born at Leeton but lived in Wagga for much of his childhood) and Michael Slater.

'WELL PLAYED, KEN . . . NOW GET OUT!'

Ken Meuleman rated his selection in Don Bradman's testimonial match (Melbourne, 1948–49) as his finest moment in cricket – even ahead of his one and only Test, in Wellington, three summers earlier. He made 100 in front of the biggest crowd of his career (53 539 spectators) and shared a century stand with the Don who, only weeks before, had been knighted for his services to cricket.

On making three figures, Meuleman was thrilled to see Bradman, his all-time cricket hero, walk down the wicket and offer his congratulations.

'Well played, Ken,' Bradman said. 'Now get out. There are other batsmen they want to see.'

'WELL, WHO DO YA WANT?'

In 1966–67, with five of its front-line players on tour with Bobby Simpson's Australians in South Africa, Victoria was a rank outsider to win the Sheffield Shield. The man entrusted to lead the state for the first time was Jack Potter, 28, a member of the 1964 team to England. The Vics were to blood six rookies in as many matches on their way to unseating the titleholders, New South Wales.

'I was asked to go to selection,' Potter said, 'and Jack Ryder [the chairman and Victorian cricket legend] said to me, "Well, who do ya want?"

'"There's only one guy that I really know I want," I said, "and that's someone who can tie up one end while we try and get them out at the other."

'I said we had this young kid at Fitzroy, Bobby Bitmead, who bowled left-arm slow [off the wrong foot] from around the wicket. "He mightn't get many wickets, but he'll tie an end up, allowing Alan Connolly and John Grant to attack downwind."

'We were playing Western Australia in Perth first-up, and they were all full of the fact that they were going to knock us off with the likes of [Tony] Lock, [Derek] Chadwick, [Laurie] Mayne, Ross Edwards and [Terry] Jenner. At the team meeting, there were some faces there I wasn't sure about (not that I let them know it). I told them that they were the best Victoria had to offer and any side Victoria had to offer was better than any side West Australia could produce because our cricket was better – and that's the way they played.

'Bobby Bitmead was one of three or four newcomers [along with Les Joslin, Eric Shade and twelfth man Peter Bedford], and I said to him to relax and enjoy himself fielding in the slips, as the wicket was green and I wasn't going to use him at all in the first innings. The last over before lunch [on the first day], I threw him the ball and he straight away took a wicket [Peter Kelly for 58]. He finished up bowling 21 overs and taking three for 26, and they didn't make even 200. We won on the first innings and went all the way, Bobby becoming a key strike bowler alongside the great Al Pal [Alan Connolly].'

A WESTERN DISTRICTS EPIC

Colac cricket identity Jim Ryan thought the worst when he received a telegram during the opening days of his Caribbean holiday, timed to take in the 1978 Jamaican Test.

'I thought someone must be crook at home,' he said. 'Then I read the contents: WARRION 410, COLAC 9/412. We'd got up. We'd won the flag!'

The bubbly lawyer had played five of the first six days of the Western Districts epic, even being promoted to No. 3, just before he and his wife, Maree, had flown out to the West Indies for the holiday of a lifetime.

'It was a final which went on and on,' he said. 'One of the early days was washed out, and they changed the rules after that so that games had to finish in no more than three days, rain or no rain.

'It was quite a celebration for us all, and a giant relief for me, as I'd dropped one of their fellas, Jimmy Gorwell, in the outfield when he was 60. He'd gone on and made 196!'

Now in his mid-sixties, and still sending down his leg-spinners for Colac's B-grade side, Ryan is in no hurry to call time.

'Maree bought me a new cricket shirt not so long ago . . . I thought that was the green light to go again for at least a couple more!' he said. 'Now I'm hoping to get some new cricket shoes. There's no grip left on my old ones, especially when the wicket gets wet.'

The still-sprightly Ryan is a regular winner of the club's bowling average and, in one spell against Irrewarra in 2003–04, sent down 18 consecutive overs, all off his super-short run-up.

'I only take two steps [before bowling], so it wasn't a real marathon,' he said. 'I still finished pretty red in the face, though. I'm always forgetting to put on my suncream.'

WHACKO JACKO

As a first-time player in England, debuting for south-of-London club Amersham in 1987, Paul Jackson was keen to show why he'd played Sheffield Shield cricket for Victoria – only to run into some local hitters who made mincemeat of him. He can't remember exactly what his figures were, but they weren't flash.

'I was hit for nine sixes on debut, and each and every one of them landed in the local peafields,' he said. 'It wasn't the way I'd hoped to have started. Call it one of my lesser performances!'

Jackson was to play 100 games at top level, for Victoria and Queensland, and while he conceded some big sixes, none embarrassed him as much as that first time on English soil in '87.

'WHAT ARE *YOU* DOING HERE? YOU'RE IN THE TEST!'

Keith Rigg was intending to spend New Year's Eve (1937) at the Peninsula Golf Club in Frankston, an hour and a half south of Melbourne's CBD. When he and his wife, Elsa, arrived in the foyer, Rigg was set upon by his friends.

'What are *you* doing here?' they asked. 'You're in the Test!'

'Elsa and I hotfooted it back to Melbourne,' remembers Rigg, 'which was quite a trip in those days. Apparently, Harry Brereton [secretary of the Victorian Cricket Association] had been trying to contact me since late in the afternoon. Unbeknown to me, two had dropped out. Both [Leo O'Brien and Arthur Chipperfield] were batsmen, so I was in.'

It was to be one of the most famous Tests of all. Witnessed by an Australian record 350 000 over the six days, Don Bradman made 270 and shared a triple-century stand with Jack Fingleton to resurrect Australia's Ashes hopes. While Rigg made only 16 and 47, his second innings contribution was particularly important, as it allowed extra time for the Melbourne wicket to dry.

'Wickets were left uncovered in those days and this was a real old-fashioned sticky,' Rigg said. 'Bradman rearranged the batting order, sending in [Bill] O'Reilly and [Chuck] Fleetwood-Smith first. It was very tricky the next morning and I was out just before lunch. In the afternoon, conditions improved and Bradman [batting at No. 7] and Fingleton [at No. 6] both made centuries, with Don going on to 270.

'It was important for us [in the morning] to occupy the crease as long as possible in the hazardous conditions. Once the wicket dried, Bradman had no problems. But if he had had to bat earlier, anything could have happened. After all, at that stage, England led 2-0 after two [matches]. The Ashes were at stake.'

With three centuries and a 97 before Christmas '37, Rigg had justified his late call-up. 'The competition [for places] from the other states made a Test place very hard to get,' he said. In the 1930–31 series against the West Indies, Rigg had been Australia's twelfth man in four Tests in a row, before finally being chosen for his maiden Test in the fifth and final match of the series, in Sydney. (He scored 14 and 16.)

WHAT MIGHT HAVE BEEN

Ron Archer had been recommended to succeed Ian Johnson as Australia's captain for the tour of South Africa in 1957–58, before fate took an untimely hand. An all-rounder of infinite promise, Archer wrenched his knee so badly after catching a spike in some matting in a Test at Karachi (1956) that he never played another international.

'I'd done a cruciate ligament and, unfortunately for me, they didn't know about them in those days,' he said. 'They put me in plaster from my ankle up for months, and it was never any good. While I had one [full] season as a batsman for Queensland, I never really played [except at Sheffield Shield level] after '56.'

During his last representative season, aged 25, Archer made 83 for Queensland against Peter May's 1958–59 Englishmen. Asked about the Test captaincy, Archer said he'd roomed with experienced Arthur Morris throughout the 1954–55 tour of the Caribbean, and the two had often discussed match strategies.

'There was a bit of a thing [talk] that I may have become the captain and that might have been part of the grooming,' he said.

With Johnson, Keith Miller and Morris all retired and Archer (a Test player at 19) suddenly out of contention, the tour of South Africa (1957–58) was led by 22-year-old Ian Craig.

Archer did captain Queensland in the absence of legendary Ray Lindwall but, being unable to bowl, he soon stopped playing altogether – an ever-so-promising Test career put permanently on hold.

WHIT'S BIG MOMENT

As No. 11 batsmen go, Mike Whitney was just about the pick of the bunch, demonstrated by his highest score of 13 and Test average of six. Any time he successfully defended a ball, applause would ring out around the ground. In Melbourne in 1987–88, even his deliberate 'leaves' were cheered, as he survived a memorable maiden over from Richard Hadlee to force a draw and ensure Australia a 1-0 series win.

'[Hadlee had] taken five-for in both innings and, quite rightly, was eyeing one final one which would have given them the match,' Whitney said. 'He must have beaten the outside edge two or three times, but somehow I survived and blocked it out. The crowd was going bananas. I walked off that day thinking how unlucky is Richard Hadlee and how lucky am I! It was the only thing I did with the bat on the cricket field. Never was there a greater moment in my [cricketing] life.'

All up, Whitney faced 18 balls and scored two not out in his 23 minutes at the crease. Craig McDermott was just as heroic, lasting 49 minutes for 10 runs.

'We'd been just five down at tea and only needing another 70 or 80 runs [to win],' said teammate Mike Veletta. 'I was in with Steve Waugh, but I went for a sweep shot against John Bracewell and it went straight on to my head and was caught in the offside field by Dipak Patel [for 39, third-top score]. Steve went out, too, and Richard Hadlee went through the rest . . . except, of course, for Whit, who played out that final over.

'There was a mixture of tension and amusement in the rooms, watching Whit let 'em go or somehow get his bat to them at the last moment. We'd won the first Test in Brisbane, so won the series. We flew to Perth that night for the start of the World Series. It was a pretty special feeling – and a nice flight.'

SEE: BATTING BUNNIES, PAGE 18

'WHO DAT NEW BOWLER, MAAN?'

It was the second day of the Federation Test match in Sydney (2000–01) and as the West Indies' No. 11, Courtney Walsh, was taking guard, Colin 'Funky' Miller was limbering up in readiness to bowl the opening over. Taking his cap off, the Funkster revealed yet another new hair colour – a warm 'Federation' blue.

'Who dat new bowler, maan?' asked Walsh, peering past the umpire.

'WHO LEADS YOU OUT TO BAT?'

Neil Harvey made 21 Test centuries for Australia – without once being able to see the scoreboard! His eyesight wasn't good enough to allow him to read anything at distance.

When the Australians were staying at the Victoria Hotel in Johannesburg, a cricket-mad optometrist whose practice was next door offered a free eye-test to all members of the team.

'We had an hour to kill and in I went,' said Harvey. 'He put the chart up there and I gave him some funny answers, which obviously weren't right. He said, "Listen, come back tomorrow and have another go."

'I sat in the same chair [the next day], looked at the card and gave him the same set of wrong answers. "Tell me, Neil," he said. "Your eyes aren't that brilliant. Who leads you out to bat?"

'He organised some glasses for me and, for the first time, I could see the ball going backwards and forwards from one end to the other! I'd wear them to the movies, but not for any outside stuff. I think I was too vain to do that. I also figured I'd done reasonably well without them, so why worry?'

SEE: NEIL HARVEY'S FINEST HOUR, PAGE 137

WHOOPS

Doug Walters once slept in before a Test match in the Caribbean (1973) and didn't arrive at Sabina Park until 20 minutes into the first session.

'It won't happen again, will it, Doug?' said captain Ian Chappell.

'Actually, Ian,' said Walters, 'I can't promise that.'

SEE: THE BRIEFEST OF NETS, PAGE 33

WIDE-EYED AND AFFABLE

Don Bradman farewelled Test cricket in 1947–48 with four centuries against the touring Indians, plus his hundredth century in a tour match in Sydney. The Indians were wide-eyed and affable, losing four Tests and drawing one through rain. They did, however, boast some highly competent cricketers, like world-class all-rounder Vinoo Mankad.

Not only was Mankad the first of the tourists to make a century against the Australians, he surrounded himself in controversy by running out opening batsman Bill Brown twice, when Brown backed up too far at the non-striker's end. One of nature's gentlemen, Brown says Mankad was totally within his rights, even though he hadn't knowingly been trying to take an advantage.

'The first time was in [the second Test in] Sydney and the other time was in Melbourne, for an Australian XI versus the Indians,' Brown said. '[In Sydney] we were having a drink at Usher's hotel with Ian Johnson, Lindsay [Hassett] and a few of the boys. They said to me, "Bill, Vinoo's not a bad sort of a bloke. He's just staying down the road at The Australia. Why don't you ring him and ask if he wants to have a drink?"

'So I did. I rang him.

'"Vinoo Mankad here."

'"Bill Brown here, Vinoo." There was dead silence. I think he thought I was really going to tear strips off him. "There are a few of us here at Usher's. Why don't you come and have a drink with us?"

'"No," he said. "I do not drink."

'"Come and have a soft one, then?"

'"No, if you don't mind, I will not. But I'll tell you this, Bill. I'll never do that to you again."

'We went to Melbourne, and I'd made 99 and was batting with Neil Harvey when he hit one square on the offside. It was touch and go, and the fellow at point threw the wicket down and I was out by a couple of feet.

'As I walked off, I wondered who the dead-eye dick was at point. I looked around to see, and it was Vinoo!'

THE WINDSOR, TO START WITH

You can imagine Arthur Morris's excitement when first chosen, at 16, to represent the New South Wales second XI in Melbourne. He was still in fourth form at Canterbury Boys' High School and had never been out of Sydney.

'There was an initial hiccup, though,' he said. 'My father thought I'd have to pay and told me he wouldn't let me go. Then he found out that they gave us one pound a day for expenses, first-class train travel, and [that we] were stopping at the Hotel Windsor!

'It wasn't a bad hotel to start with . . . I'd never ever been in a hotel before. But I've been in a few since!'

X
||||||||||||

THE X-FACTOR

Having amassed 2500 career wickets, a dozen centuries and 'eight or nine' first XI premierships, Tommy Lloyd remains one of the Western District's ultimate cricket legends. He was the X-factor at Colac Cricket Club for 40 years; his three differently paced wrong 'uns snared him dozens of wickets.

Ironically, Tommy had been a fast bowler into his mid-twenties. But, on hot practice nights, he'd often start off a long run-up before slowing down and experimenting with a variety of off-breaks and leggies.

'One day, we'd hardly got any wickets, and the skipper said, "You'd better try those leggies of yours." I got five or six [wickets] that day and never bowled the faster stuff again.'

As a 14-year-old, Tommy had taken eight for 2 in only his fourth A-grade game, bowling medium-pace. His best analysis as a leg-spinner was eight for 9. His finest year came in 1967–68 when he averaged 100 with the bat and took 69 wickets (average 8.25) in 10 home and away games and two finals. In all matches that summer, he took more than 100 wickets.

In his late sixties and still competitive in lawn bowls, Tommy was asked how he was enjoying his adopted sport.

'Oh, it's okay. I enjoy it,' he said.

'Is it as good as cricket?'

'Nothing is as good as cricket, and I mean *nothing*!'

SEE: BROTHERS WITH ARMS, PAGE 36

X-RATED

England opener Dennis Amiss was Public Enemy No. 1, at least for Dennis Lillee during the 1974–75 Ashes contests. Lillee made a habit of being as provocative as possible and, in addition to his near-express outswing and bounce, he handed out stares and sledges. Amiss fell five times to him in six Tests. One day, Amiss asked Lillee to repeat a verbal salvo, as he hadn't understood a word of the first offering. The second, longer and even more x-rated, would have puzzled even a linguistics expert.

Amiss said both Lillee and Jeff Thomson were fast, furious and on a mission to hurt as many of the English as possible. Asked later if the swearing had affected him, he said, 'No, I was never out there long enough!'

y

||||||||||||

YEARS BEFORE HIS TIME

The 1955 Australians left Sydney, bound for the West Indies, at lunchtime one early-autumn Saturday. Their first stopover was Nandi in Fiji. After eight hours in the air, Billy Watson was particularly keen to stretch his legs and dashed off towards the airport shop, looking for a newspaper.

'Just want to see the Sydney grade scores!' he said.

'YOU ALWAYS GET OUT LIKE THAT, FAVELL!'

Les Favell was a marvellous, magnetic personality. He was particularly loved at the Adelaide Oval, where he would sail into the bowling, much in the fashion of an Adam Gilchrist or an Andrew Symonds.

Les hadn't played for almost a decade when he agreed to play one last match, for Old South Australia against Old Victoria at the Adelaide Oval, in the mid-eighties. While Les was well into his fifties, he still had an eagle-eye and, taking block against Gary Cosier, he went *whack, whack, whack* and reached double figures in no time, before hoisting an intended lofted drive high to mid-on. It was midweek in Adelaide and, as Favell was walking off, one solitary spectator standing on the old northern bank yelled, 'You always get out like that, Favell!'

YOU HAVEN'T GOT IT, SON

Mike Tamblyn just shrugs his shoulders now, when he hears of Shane Warne's latest wicket-taking record. As Brighton's second XI captain in the mid-eighties, Tamblyn told a teenage Warne – in his first summer of open-age cricket – that he should concentrate on his batting rather than his leg-spinners.

'Shane had just turned 17 and didn't bowl the same stuff [as now]. He bowled an occasional offie and even a slow-medium [pacer] thrown in there as well,' Tamblyn said. 'He used to flick them across his fingers and could move the ball off the seam . . . but I was more impressed by his batting. He always stuck around when I wanted him to, wherever he batted.'

Wicketkeeper George Voyage was more impressed, however. 'He had a real loop to his bowling, even then,' he said of Warne.

Warne took 12 wickets in eight games at Brighton, including three in his maiden first XI match, when he bowled in tandem with the club's playing coach and county-standard bowler, Ole Mortensen. Warne joined St Kilda in 1987, beginning one of the most illustrious careers ever.

'YOU SHOULD HAVE TAKEN THE MONEY'

Shane Warne was in a beachside casino in Colombo, playing roulette. And losing. Red 23 wasn't proving as lucky as normal. When a man Mark Waugh had introduced him to at the tables offered $US5000 as a token of appreciation to cover his losses, Warne was initially hesitant. But he took the envelope and shook hands, unaware that the man smiling back at him was an Indian bookmaker offering a deadly sweetener.

Not only had Warne inadvertently become a participant in the illegal billion-dollar cricket gambling industry, within a month he and spin partner Tim May were targeted for the biggest sting of all – the throwing of a Test match in Karachi. They refused, Australia lost by a single wicket and, on the victory podium, Pakistan's captain Saleem 'The Rat' Malik – part of the betting ring – hissed at man-of-the-match Warne, 'You should have taken the money.'

A YOUNG TORNADO

When West Australian opener Ric Charlesworth first faced a young Jeff Thomson, he felt decidedly lonely.

'The 'keeper, John Maclean, was a long, long way away and the slips were standing closer to the fence than they were to me. "Are you okay back there?" I called.

'"Yeah mate, we know what we're doin'."

'Soon, I realised why. Thommo was lightning and I was out cheaply to him both times, nicking the ball through to Maclean. The only runs I made came from snicks which flew *over* the slips. If anything, they were all too close!'

'YOU'RE OUT, MATE'

Mel Johnson smiled more than most umpires. He genuinely felt he had the best seat in the house from 22 yards – and when you're watching world-class players, why not enjoy yourself? One day, a batsman lingered after being on the end of what he considered a poor decision.

'You're out, mate,' said Johnson.

'How?' asked the batsman, who just happened to be Allan Border.

'I don't know . . . Just piss off!'

YOUR SERVE, SIR!

In a tour match at the WACA Ground, England's Darren Gough told Justin Langer he wasn't half the player Matthew Hayden was.

'If you thought Aussies were meant to be bad sledgers, then you should have heard Gough going off his head this day,' Langer said. 'I took his stares and insults for only so long before I told him he had an ego the size of the Lillee-Marsh Stand [at the WACA].

'He then told me I was only a very average player, I shouldn't even have been playing Test cricket, and that I'd better look out for the likes of [Greg] Blewett, [Matthew] Elliott and [Matthew] Hayden, because they were all far better players than I would ever be.'

More than a dozen Test centuries later, including one of the fastest on record by an Australian against New Zealand [Hamilton, 1999–2000], Langer continued to defy the non-believers. He and fellow left-hander Hayden built one of the finest records of any opening pair, including legendary Englishmen Jack Hobbs and Herbert Sutcliffe.

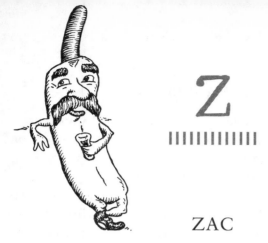

Z

||||||||||||

ZAC

As a teenager, Harry Zachariah took five wickets in an innings against the 1930–31 West Indians in a match at Corio Oval. (The match was notable, also, for an unbeaten century from Test captain-to-be and rising star Lindsay Hassett from Geelong College.) Included in Zachariah's haul were two of the tourists' most-celebrated: George Headley, the 'Black Bradman', and famed all-rounder Learie Constantine who, in that leisurely game, bowled five or six overs of leggies.

Tall and multi-gifted, 'Zac' thought he had a future as a medium-pacer, but he also liked to slow down and bowl spin when the ball had lost its sheen. Having switched Melbourne clubs from University to St Kilda, he was given the new ball on debut.

'Maybe I didn't get 'em quite on line but after two overs, Stuart King, our captain, marched up to me and said, "That's the last two overs you'll bowl with the new ball. You're a spin bowler . . . from now on!"'

King, one of Victoria's most notable sporting figures, had in essence relaunched Zachariah's career. The next five wartime years were to be the best and most productive of the versatile left-armer's much-travelled career. Zachariah took 274 wickets at an average of 55 a season and, along the way, shattered the records of some of St Kilda's most celebrated former bowlers, including ex-Test pair Don Blackie and Bert Ironmonger.

ZIGGING INSTEAD OF ZAGGING

John Bromwich was locked in a fierce battle with Bob Falkenburg for Wimbledon supremacy in 1948. The Australian cricket team were following every shot on television from their dressing-room at Lord's.

A wicket fell and Lindsay Hassett, still with half an eye on the match, fumbled for his bat and gloves. Out he went, only to be bowled first ball by Norman Yardley. Quickly retaking his seat, he noted Bromwich had improved his score from 15-40 to deuce. 'Deuce . . . good,' he said.

Later, he explained that he had 'zigged' instead of 'zagged' at one of Yardley's benders, but the Australians had the cricket match under control and there was far more interest in the tennis. (Bromwich lost the title in five sets, after leading five games to three and 40-15 on his serve in the fifth.)

ZIPPY AIMS FOR A BAKER'S DOZEN

Finals are a way of life for giant Gippsland paceman Steve Zimmer from Bundalaguah, who says he has been spoilt to have contested 11 A-grade grand finals. With two premierships at his original senior club, Rosedale-Kilmany, and six at Bundalaguah, 'Zippy' reckons he could amass a baker's dozen before he finishes.

'My whole career has been unforgettable,' he says. 'I've never been out of the finals . . . whether they were semifinals or grand finals.'

His work as a slaughterman in Sale gives him the extra upper-body strength that enables him to sustain his bowling hostility. The Mornington Peninsula's hall-of-famer Rob Bedford rates Zimmer as his toughest opponent and says he still has the bruises to prove it.

references

||||||||||||

BOOKS

Amiss, Dennis, *In Search of Runs* (Stanley Paul, 1976)

Andrews, Bill, *The Hand that Bowled Bradman* (Reader's Union edition, 1973)

Geddes, Margaret, *Remembering Bradman* (Penguin Australia, 2002)

Hammond, Walter, *Cricket My World* (Stanley Paul, 1948)

Langer, Justin, *The Power and the Passion* (Swan Publishing, 2002)

Mackay, Ken, *Slasher Opens Up* (Pelham Books, 1964)

McKechnie, Brian, *Double All Black* (Craig Printing Co., 1983)

Mullins, Pat & Derriman, Phil, *Bat and Pad: Writings on Australian Cricket* (Oxford University Press, 1984)

Pollock, Peter, *God's Own Fast Bowler* (Christian Art Publishers, 2001)

Tennyson, Lord Lionel, *Sticky Wickets* (Christopher Johnson, 1950)

Webster, Ray, *First-Class Cricket in Australia*, Vols 1 & 2 (self-published, 1991 & 1997)

Whitington, R. S., *Keith Miller, the Golden Nugget* (Rigby, 1981)

Wisden Cricketers' Almanack

MAGAZINES

Australian Cricket (Mason Stewart/Emap, Sydney)

Cricketer (Newspress, Melbourne)

INTERNET

www.bushrangers.com.au

www.cricketbooks.com.au

index

||||||||||||

INDEX

INDEX

INDEX

COVER PHOTOS
Top: Classic cricket in the park: South Yarra v. Emmanuel South Oakleigh, Fawkner Park, Melbourne, 2002 (Andy Campbell is the wicket-taker)
Centre: Time for a coldie: Mercantile Cricket Association Over 40s v. Under 21s, 2004 (Photographs © Robyn Campbell, The Melbourne Headshot Company)
Bottom: Australian legends (from left): Bill Johnston, Dennis Lillee, Norman O'Neill